AVIATION READERS

Airplanes at Work

By
GERTRUDE WHIPPLE

—————

THE MACMILLAN COMPANY · NEW YORK

CONTENTS

U. S. Forest Service

This plane flying over the forest is like the one Sam flies.

CHAPTER I

FIGHTING FIRE FROM THE AIR

The Flying Lookout

This bright sunny morning Sam is flying a small, yellow airplane over the forest. As he flies along, he looks down at the trees which grow for miles and miles below him.

The young pilot sees a path winding around a mountain up to a big rock near the top.

The trees grow so close together that Sam sees only their tops. They grow down in the valleys and up the sides of the mountains. Even the tops of the low mountains are covered with trees.

The pilot looks for smoke as he flies along. He knows that the leaves under

1

the trees are dry, for there has been little rain for weeks. The leaves would take fire easily.

Suddenly Sam sees some smoke rising straight ahead of him. When he is right above the smoke, he sees a smoldering fire. As he looks, a flame flashes up. If this fire is not stopped, it will burn quickly through the dry leaves. Then the trees will catch fire. If there is a wind, it will blow the flames along.

The plane has a radio through which the pilot can talk to men on the ground. Now Sam speaks over this radio to the ranger who cares for the forest.

"Fire on the east side of Deer Mountain near Big Rock," Sam says to the ranger.

The ranger hears Sam's voice through his head phones. Though he is far away, he talks to Sam about the fire.

2

Sam's radio is different from the radios which we use in our homes. He uses it like a telephone. This kind of radio is called a two-way radio.

Through his radio, Sam hears the ranger ask, "How many fire fighters are needed?"

"Two if they come at once," answers Sam. "Trees are just beginning to burn. It will not take many men to keep the blaze from spreading."

Then the pilot circles about in his plane to watch the fire until the fighters come. He hopes that they will be there soon.

Sam owns his yellow plane. It is a small plane and does not use as much gasoline as a large plane would. Sam is hired to fly over this part of the forest and look for smoke. On the days when he works, he makes three or four trips over the forest. Our government owns this big forest and does not want the trees to be burned. Someone must be on watch for fires in the forest all the time. We say that Sam patrols the forest.

In some parts of this forest a ranger watches for fires from a little tower high up on a mountain. A man must be in the tower every hour of the day. When he sees smoke, he sends word to the head ranger, just as Sam did. Then the ranger sends fire fighters to stop the fire.

There are many places in the forest which cannot be seen from the lookout towers. The pilot is paid to patrol these parts of the forest. Because he is higher up in the air, he can see more of the forest than a ranger can see from the tower.

When Sam stops work, another pilot

Here is a fire running through a forest. It burns the leaves, bushes, and trees. The fire Sam found would have become big like this one if he had not called the fire fighters.

is ready to take Sam's place and fly over the forest to watch for fires. In hot weather someone must patrol the forest every hour of the day. Leaves and twigs that have fallen to the ground are very dry and would catch fire easily.

If a fire is found soon after it has started, the fire fighters can soon put it out. If it gets to be a big fire, it will burn many trees down. Then the wood of the trees cannot be used. It takes many men to fight a big fire. These men must leave their other work.

Pilots like Sam help to protect the forests which our government owns. They also patrol other forests in our country which are not owned by the government. Some of the wood from these forests is used to make paper, and some of it is used as lumber to build houses and to make furniture and other things. The large forests in our country must be patrolled in dry weather. Fliers who look for fires in our forests are doing very important work.

Mr. Smoke Jumper

The fire which Sam has seen is in a thick part of the forest far from good roads. Fire fighters cannot reach it easily by truck. If they should ride on horses or mules, it would take them many hours to get there. In the meantime the fire would spread. It would get bigger and bigger and would burn many trees to ashes. It would kill many wild animals and birds.

But the forest ranger knows how to get fire fighters to Deer Mountain in a short time. Already an airplane is speeding through the sky carrying two fighters.

The pilot of this plane is named John. The two other young men, Bill and Slim, are called smoke jumpers. They know how to jump out of a plane and land on the ground without getting hurt.

Bill is dressed in his smoke-jumping suit. It has thick pads to protect him against trees and rocks. Across the

U. S. Forest Service

This is a fire fighter like Bill in his smoke-jumping suit. He is wearing his helmet but has not put on the mask which will protect his face. In the picture on page 16 you can see what the mask looks like.

8

front of his suit he wears a pack which looks like a pillow. It has cords across it and straps which go over his shoulders. There are straps under his arms and around his waist, too. He has another pack on his back.

Soon you will find out how Bill uses these packs when he jumps from the plane. If he drops into a pine tree, he will not be hurt. The branches will not scratch his face because he wears a helmet and mask to protect him. His helmet covers his ears and comes down almost to his eyes. The collar of his jacket comes up almost to his mouth. You can see just a little bit of Bill's smiling face between his helmet and his collar. When he gets ready to jump from the plane, he will put a wire mask over his face. When he jumps, Bill carries a coil of light, strong rope. If he lands in a tall tree, he can use this rope in getting down to the ground. He has a radio in a little box.

Slim looks like a football player in his padded suit. You cannot see much of him because of his smoke-jumping suit.

When the men come in sight of the fire, John points at it and grins at Bill. They are old friends and have gone to many fires together. They have not known Slim very long. He is a new man, but John and Bill think that they will like him.

The plane's engine makes a great deal of noise. The pilot flies as fast as he can, for the men want to get to the fire quickly.

Then John points to Sam's plane over Deer Mountain. When Sam sees that the fire fighters have come, he flies away to patrol another part of the forest. He

This man is dropping a bundle from a plane. See the cans of food
for the fire fighters.

keeps looking for smoke and flies around
until it is time for him to go back to the
landing field.

Bill moves to the doorway of the
plane, which is large and has no door.

11

"Let her go!" calls John. Bill drops a bundle out the doorway. He is careful to drop it so that it will fall in a spot where the fire is not burning.

As the men watch the bundle fall, a long yellow streamer stretches out. A parachute pops out of the bundle and fills with air until it looks like an umbrella.

John banks his plane, or rolls it over on one side, to see where the bundle lands. It reaches the ground a little way from the fire. Bill sees that it has fallen in a safe place. The pilot has reached the right spot for the fire fighters to jump out of the plane. He pulls his plane out of the roll and lets it fly level again.

"Now!" he shouts.

Bill steps to the doorway and holds to the side. Then John, who is watch-

A man has just jumped from this plane. Do you see the small parachute which slows up the jumper's fall and opens up the big parachute?

ing Bill, nods his head. Bill smiles and plunges headfirst as if he were diving into a swimming pool.

Bill counts to himself as he falls, "One, two, three, four, five." Now he knows that he is clear of the plane. He reaches to his chest and takes hold of a ring which is fastened by a cord to the

13

These men have just jumped from a plane and are falling toward a forest fire. Which one jumped out first?

pack on his back. Bill jerks the cord, which is called the rip-cord, and a parachute is pulled out of the pack. The air catches and fills the parachute, and it opens up above Bill's head.

The parachute sways in the wind. Heavy cords go from this parachute to the straps over Bill's shoulders and chest. Now Bill's head is up, and his feet are down.

The parachute makes Bill fall more slowly. If he falls too fast, he will be hurt as he hits the ground. He swings and sways in the air as he comes down.

Bill wants to land near the bundle. He pulls on the lines at one side of his parachute. It tips above him and lets out some of the air. The parachute changes its direction.

Down, down Bill goes. As he falls, he looks at the land below him. He sees where his bundle has fallen. The tops of the trees come close. He smells the smoke from the fire. Bill keeps his arms close to his body. He keeps his feet together. If he had not changed his direction, he might have fallen among the burning trees.

Swish! Bill lands in a tree. But the

This jumper has just landed among the trees. His parachute has
caught in a tree

16

branches do not hurt him because he has on his jumper's suit. Now he slips out of the tree easily to reach solid ground. The dry leaves rustle and crack under his feet.

It has taken Bill only a few minutes to fall. He waves a streamer in the air to let John know that he has landed safely.

Then Bill turns around. Slim is just a little way from him.

The men loosen the harnesses which hold their parachutes. They pull the zippers on their jumping suits and step out of them. They toss their helmets to the ground and push through the underbrush till they reach their bundles with the yellow streamers. There are two bundles, for Slim threw one out, too.

John's plane circles above the fire. He sees that the smoke jumpers have landed safely. For a while he circles about to watch the fire. If he sees it breaking out in a new place, he will talk to Bill and Slim over their two-way radios.

Now Bill and Slim can begin to fight the fire.

You can see what is in Bill's open bundle. He has a shovel, a hatchet, an axe, a rake, and other fire-fighting tools. There is a first-aid kit in case the men burn themselves. There is food for them to eat when they get hungry. There is drinking water in a can with a top that screws on.

Slim and Bill begin to chop a wide path, or fire trail, around the fire. Slash, slash, slash go their axes as they cut away the trees and bushes. The men work fast. They must keep the fire from spreading. It is jumping from

18

U. S. Forest Service

This fire was not found soon enough. So it is spreading fast. Which way is the wind blowing the fire? What harm do you think this fire will do?

tree to tree. A burning tree falls. It swishes down into the brush, and the flames seem to eat it up.

The fire fighters are cleaning the brush away from a strip of land on one side of the fire. Then the fire will not spread in that direction, for there will be nothing to burn on the bare earth.

Now Slim reaches for one end of a tool called a pick. It has a long wooden handle. At one end of the handle is a curved iron bar with sharp ends. Slim digs up the tough bushes with his pick. He raises the pick over his head. Then he drives the sharp point into the ground. As a bush comes up by the roots, he throws it to the side away from the fire. "This strip is clear enough," he says.

The men are thirsty. Bill reaches for his can of water. He takes off the lid to get a drink. His face is dripping with sweat. The sleeves of his blue shirt are rolled up. Sweat drips from his arms. But he grins at Slim as he screws the top on the can.

"Hot work," Slim says as he reaches for his can of water. "But it won't be

20

long!" Slim coughs and sputters. The smoke makes his throat dry. His eyes sting.

John is still flying his plane in a circle above the fire. Now he talks over his radio to Slim and Bill.

"Hey, boys! The fire is breaking out on the south. Look out, there!"

The smoke jumpers push their way through the underbrush to the south end of the fire. They cut away the brush and dig up the roots. They make a wide path beyond the fire and save many trees.

"There, that ought to hold it," says Slim.

Soon there is a wide path of bare ground entirely around the fire. The fire fighters have done their work. They have not put out the fire, but they have cut a path around it. The bare ground will keep the fire from burning the rest of the forest. Unless a strong wind comes up and sweeps the flames across the path, the fire will die out.

When the men stop to rest, they hear John speaking to them from the plane.

"Good work, fellows! Bill, you had better stay and watch this fire for a while. Slim, you can meet me at the landing field."

Bill stays to watch while the fire dies down. He will eat his lunch here and will not leave until the last spark of fire is out.

Slim picks up his lunch and tools and makes his way slowly through the thick woods.

At last Slim comes to a place where all the trees have been cut down. John's plane has already landed there. The men sit down under a tree to eat.

"This is a good landing field," Slim says to John, as he looks about him. "Why couldn't you have landed us here and saved us our jump?"

"I could," John agrees. "But it's a long walk from here to where the fire was beginning. Your tools would have been pretty heavy if you had carried them on your back as you hurried to the fire. You would have been too tired to fight the fire."

"I guess you're right," Slim says.

"I kept watching the fire," the pilot tells Slim. "If it had been a big fire, I would have gone for more fighters. Once we had to bring eight men to a fire. But you and Bill took care of this one."

"We had to work pretty fast," Slim says. "It's a good thing there isn't a wind today."

Sometimes small fires begin in several places at once. The fires in this picture were started by lightning. See the wing of the plane. A man in this plane sees the fires before they burn very long.

" A strong wind can blow a fire right through a forest. Hundreds of fighters are sometimes needed to keep a fire from spreading in a high wind."

" Now I'd better take off and fly you back," John says. "The ranger may have more work for you. Bill will watch this fire and let us know when it's out. Then I'll come back for him."

There are many parts of this forest which are easily reached by roads and trails. If a fire breaks out in any of these places, the ranger can send most of the fire fighters by truck. The trucks bring fire-fighting tools. They bring food and water for the men, for sometimes the fire fighters must work for many days and nights. If the fire is burning fast when the lookout first sees it, the ranger may send some smoke jumpers.

As you know, airplanes travel faster than trucks. So smoke jumpers always reach the fire before the men in the trucks can get there. Airplanes help us to save many trees.

The Fire Scout

The next morning John, the pilot, is at home eating his breakfast. His wife has cooked his favorite sausages. He has just taken a mouthful of sausage when the telephone rings. Laying his napkin on the table, he chews his food quickly as he moves toward the phone and picks it up.

"Hello!" he says.

"This is Jim," says the ranger's voice over the phone. "The fire in Bear Hollow has spread. Fifty men are working on it, and I am sending more. Will you take a plane and help direct the men from the air? Bill can go along with you."

"Yes," replies John. "I'll be right there!"

John goes back to the table and stands while he drinks his coffee. He puts a piece of sausage between two slices of bread and wraps the sandwich in paper.

"I'll finish my breakfast as I drive to the landing field," he says to his wife.

"Will you put up a lunch for me? And don't look for me till late afternoon."

John quickly puts on his working suit, puts the sandwich in his pocket, and takes the lunch box his wife has packed for him. Though he had expected to have the day off, he is soon driving to the flying field. There Bill is waiting for him. A mechanic, or man who takes care of machines, says the plane is ready.

Bill and John climb into the plane. John starts the engine and with a swift take-off is soon in the air. Bear Hollow, the ranger had said.

As the plane nears Bear Hollow, Bill sees blue smoke hanging over it like a blanket. On the sides of the hills flames are racing from tree to tree. "Looks like a bad fire," Bill says. "Wind must have come up and fanned the flames."

John looks out at the fire and shakes his head. "It's spreading fast, Bill. We'll circle around it, and then you can decide the best way for us to help."

The fire fighters down on the ground are clearing trails as fast as they can, but the fire is getting ahead of them. They do not know how fast the fire is burning and cannot see where new trails need to be cut. No roads or streams are close by to stop the fire.

Bill tries to speak over his radio to the fire boss on the ground, but the boss does not answer him. Quickly Bill writes a note telling that the fire is burning fast down the slope of the mountain. Several fighters should be sent ahead of the fire to cut a trail across its path.

Then John flies the plane toward the spot where Bill wants to drop the note.

This big fire is like the one which Bill directed from the plane.
The smoke goes high up above the earth into the air.

The men watch it fall and see a little
parachute open above it. It floats slowly
to the ground.

John banks his plane and circles over
the fire. Bill looks down and sees one
of the men pick up the note and read it.

Far below, the men begin to move
around the fire. The fire boss knows
now where to place his men. He knows

where they can work safely and not be caught by the fire. He says to his men, " Cut a trail on the slope ahead of the fire."

Now Bill sees the men scatter out and begin to work as he has told them. As John's plane circles around above the fire, Bill hopes the fighters can get ahead of the flames. He wants to help the men make their work count.

Bill keeps on watching, for he must help the boss until the fire is stopped. He notices that the wind begins to blow from another direction. He sees bright flames springing up in new places.

Bill is puzzled. Will the fire change its direction? Will other parts of the forest be in danger of burning?

Then he smiles. He sees what the fire fighters must do. He writes another note. It, too, drops down under a little parachute. The fire fighters are sent off in another direction to try to stop the fire.

"That is a good move," John says. "There's a chance that the men can stop it."

"Yes, I think they can," Bill says. "The wind seems to be slowing down. Anyway, the fire isn't spreading as fast as it was."

The plane keeps on circling above the fire. John has to stay high in the air because of the heat and smoke.

A little later, John sees that his gasoline is getting low. He talks to the head ranger over the radio. The ranger tells him to return to the flying field. He says that Sam will come to take John's place if the fire spreads again.

But John knows that Sam is needed to patrol other parts of the forest. He tells the ranger he will fly back for gas and return quickly to the fire. Then John remembers the lunch his wife put up for him. As he flies back, he opens the lunch box and eats a sandwich and an apple. Then he has some cookies and drinks milk from a small bottle. Bill eats his lunch, too.

As soon as the gas tank has been filled, John and Bill return. They keep flying above the fire. Now and then Bill drops a note to the men.

John and Bill keep directing the fire fighters far into the night. There is no moon, but the fire lights up that part of the forest until it is almost as bright as day. About midnight the ranger tells John over the radio that another pilot is coming to take John's place. That pilot also has an observer, or scout, like Bill.

Then John and Bill fly back to the home

field. They climb wearily out of the plane, and a mechanic takes charge of it.

" You did a fine job today," John says, clapping Bill on the shoulder.

" You did your share, too," answers Bill.

The two men part and go home to sleep the rest of the night.

Sometimes a fire scout like Bill tells the fire boss the shortest way for his men to reach a fire. In rough country where there are few trails, it is hard for the fire fighters to find the easiest way in.

Sometimes the scout takes a picture of the fire from the plane. He makes the picture while he is up in the plane. This does not take long. When the picture is ready, he drops it to the fire boss. The boss studies the picture to see where the land is high and low. He sees that in some places there are trees and bushes which will burn fast and in other places there are plants which will not burn so fast. He sees where there are streams, roads, and trails. He can see all this much more quickly than he could if he had to walk around the fire. He can see it more clearly, too.

QUESTIONS TO TALK OVER

1. How do airplanes help forest rangers to fight fires?
2. What kind of plane is best for patrolling a forest? Why?
3. How does a patrol pilot talk with a ranger?
4. Does a pilot fly fast when he takes smoke jumpers to a fire? Why?
5. What kind of man do you think would make a good smoke jumper? Give reasons for your answer.
6. What kind of man do you think would make a good fire scout? Give reasons for your answer.

THINGS TO DO

1. Find out other ways in which airplanes are used in our large forests. They are used in some ways which were not told in these stories.

2. Make a drawing to fit one of the following names and write the name below your picture.

A plane patrolling a forest.

Two smoke jumpers about to take off in a plane.

A smoke jumper's bundle coming down.

A smoke jumper in his parachute nearing the ground.

A smoke jumper whose parachute is caught in a tree.

Men cutting a fire trail in a forest.

When all the pictures are finished, they may be shown to the entire class. Talk over the pictures to see which ones agree best with the stories you have read.

3. Bring to class pictures of airplanes used in fire fighting. Show them to your classmates.

4. Visit an airport to see any small airplanes there which do not use much gasoline. Is there one like Sam's plane?

WORDS TO EXPLAIN

pilot	patrol (the forest)	parachute
smoke jumper	two-way radio	mask
observer	helmet	smoke-jumping
fire scout	fire trail	suit
mechanic	bank (a plane)	rip-cord

Can you find the stewardess in this picture? Do you see anyone
else who works for the airlines? What is he doing?

CHAPTER II

CARRYING PASSENGERS, MAIL, AND EXPRESS

Flying West

This afternoon Mr. Roberts comes rushing out of his house in New York City to a taxi which has just stopped in the drive. He carries a black leather suitcase.

"To La Guardia Airport," he says to the driver. "I must be on time for the afternoon plane to Los Angeles. It leaves in just half an hour."

The taxi goes rapidly down the street. Mr. Roberts carries a copy of the afternoon paper. Now and then he takes his watch out of his pocket to see what time it is.

Mr. Roberts is going on a business trip. He is manager of a New York factory which makes parts for airplanes. In Los Angeles he will see the manager of a factory which also makes parts for airplanes.

Since Mr. Roberts is a busy man, he wants to reach Los Angeles quickly. He also wants to return to New York as soon as possible. That is why he will travel at night.

At the airport the taxi driver gives Mr. Roberts' suitcase to a porter. The porter follows Mr. Roberts to the ticket window and waits while he buys his ticket. Then the suitcase is weighed. Each passenger is allowed to carry forty pounds of baggage. If he wants to carry more, he must pay extra. But Mr. Roberts' suitcase weighs less than forty pounds. He is given a small bag in

These people are boarding a plane at night.

which to put the things he will need for the night. He takes a few things from his suitcase and puts them into the little bag. Now his suitcase is ready to be put on the Los Angeles plane. He waits at a gate to the landing field.

In a very few minutes a silver and blue plane moves up near the gates. There are windows on each side of the

39

cabin. The passengers can look out of these windows. In the front is the pilot's cabin, or cockpit. It is large enough for two pilots.

Now the gate is opened, and the passengers walk out to the plane. Mr. Roberts carries the small bag as he goes up a little stairway to the door. The stewardess stands at the door to greet the passengers and check them in. She asks each person's name and then checks that name on her list. This pleasant young woman has a smile for the passengers. She is dressed in a blue suit with a little blue hat tilted over her forehead. As she checks off Mr. Roberts' name, he steps into the plane and looks for his seat number.

Mr. Roberts finds his seat far back in the plane. He sinks into a big, cushioned seat and looks around. Other passengers enter the plane, and soon all the seats are filled. Then the door is closed.

The plane begins to move along the runway. A runway is a strip of pavement or hard ground on which planes land and take off. There are many long, straight runways on this field. The plane goes faster and faster, and before it reaches the middle of the long runway, it rises into the air.

The cabin in which Mr. Roberts sits has many seats. There are electric lights near each seat so that the passengers can read. The air is neither too hot nor too cold. There are windows at the side of each row of seats. The inside of the plane is like a long narrow room or the inside of a railway sleeping car before the berths, or beds, are made up.

In the back part of the cabin is a galley, or small kitchen. When evening comes,

Here is a stewardess serving a tray in her galley. She gets the food out of cans which keep it either hot or cold.

the stewardess brings the passengers their dinner from this galley. The food was prepared in kitchens at the airport before the plane left the ground. Then it was put into big cans or bottles which keep the food hot. Other cans and bottles like these keep food and water cold.

The stewardess places a table before Mr. Roberts. She sets the table with linen, silver, and dishes. Then she serves his dinner of hot chicken pie, steaming vegetables, hot rolls, and a green salad. Later she brings him ice cream and coffee. Mr. Roberts does not have to pay extra for this meal. The stewardess serves all the other passengers, too.

After dinner, Mr. Roberts leans back in his seat and reads a magazine. Some of the other passengers on the plane talk. Others read. A few play cards, write letters, or look out of the window. The stewardess takes care of a baby so that its mother can rest and enjoy her trip.

It does not seem to Mr. Roberts that the plane is going fast or that it is high up in the air. Now and then he looks out of

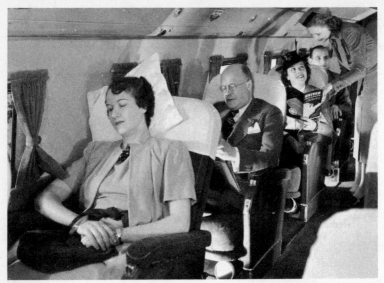

United Air Lines

This picture shows the chairs in which passengers sit. This plane
does not have berths, but the comfortable chairs may be tipped
back. What is the stewardess doing?

the window to see if the plane is flying
over a city. Sometimes he sees the head-
light of a train.

Late that evening the stewardess makes
up a lower berth for Mr. Roberts. She
lets down the backs of the seats and puts
the mattress on top. The berth has a

This is the kind of berth in which Mr. Roberts slept. He has two windows in his berth.

soft mattress and snowy white sheets. Curtains shut the bed off from the rest of the cabin just as in a railway sleeping car. Above Mr. Roberts' berth is another just like his. The stewardess lets down a movable part near the top of the wall and makes it up as a berth for another passenger.

Mr. Roberts takes off his coat and hangs it up. He goes to the men's room at the back of the plane to wash. When he returns, he pulls the curtains together and puts on his pajamas. Then he gets into bed, fastens the seat belt over him, turns off the lights, and goes to sleep.

Some of the passengers stay up a long time after Mr. Roberts has gone to bed. They sit in the front of the plane talking quietly. Some play games.

During the night the plane stops two or three times at landing fields to fill the gas tanks and let passengers on or off. Usually it lands and takes off so gently that Mr. Roberts is not awakened.

In the morning another stewardess wakes Mr. Roberts Since the crew, or persons who run the plane, do not work more than eight hours at a time, the plane has changed crews during the night. Now the plane is nearing Los Angeles. "Is it eight o'clock already?" asks Mr. Roberts.

"Almost. You may have your breakfast as soon as you are ready."

After dressing Mr. Roberts goes to the men's room. He washes and shaves. When he goes back to the cabin, the stewardess has made up his berth.

He is ready for breakfast, and now a hot meal is set before him. He has a good appetite and enjoys the food. Then he leans back in his seat and looks out the window. The sky is clear and blue.

Already the plane has passed over the mountains and is flying along a valley with mountains or hills on each side. The plane is flying low enough for Mr. Roberts to see groves of fruit trees and highways leading to the city. He can see Los Angeles and small towns near by. Farther on he sees the blue ocean.

In the front of the cabin, a sign is lighted which says, " Fasten Seat Belt." It is not long until the plane starts to come down. Mr. Roberts reaches for the seat belt. He fastens it around him so that he will be safe while the plane lands. The other passengers also fasten their seat belts.

In the front of the cabin, the " No Smoking " sign is lighted. Passengers must not smoke during landings and take-offs.

Soon the plane is in the Los Angeles airport. Mr. Roberts picks up his hat and the little bag. As he leaves the plane, he thanks the stewardess for a pleasant trip. He passes through the waiting room to the car which will take him and other passengers downtown. His suitcase is put into the car and will be given to him when he reaches his hotel.

Mr. Roberts has crossed our country overnight. Yesterday he was in New York.

The airlines have cars ready to take passengers to and from the air field. In New York Mr. Roberts could have gone to the airport in a car like this if he had been downtown.

Today he is in Los Angeles. He is ready to make his business visits, and he has lost no working time. He arrives rested and ready for work.

The silver and blue plane is at the end of its trip. Later it will carry passengers back to New York. But before it does so,

49

it must be inspected and cleaned from nose to tail.

When our country is at war, persons who need to travel on important war work have the first right to travel by plane. Other people do not have a chance to ride unless there are empty seats. Sleeper planes such as that on which Mr. Roberts rode do not run in time of war. Sometimes a passenger may be asked to give up his seat to someone who is traveling on war business.

In the Cockpit

Charles Harris is pilot of a plane which travels across our country. His plane is much like the one on which Mr. Roberts spent the night. Harris is a strong young man twenty-seven years old. He learned to be a pilot after he finished college.

This evening Harris is high in the nose

American Airlines, Inc.

What are these men doing? Find a cargo pit in the picture.

of his plane at the La Guardia Airport. It is raining hard. The sides of the silver plane glisten as it stands in front of the waiting room. Men load express packages and sacks of mail into a front part of the fuselage, or body. Here are inclosed places called cargo pits. Freight, or cargo, is carried in the pits. The cargo of this plane is made up of baggage, mail, and express. There are also cargo pits at the back of the plane.

Now passengers go up the steps into the plane. They close their wet umbrellas, and the stewardess greets them as they enter. She shuts the door, and the steps are rolled away.

Beside one wing of the plane stands the dispatcher. He is the man who will give the signal that all is clear. The co-pilot, Ben Smith, who is in the cockpit, looks down at the dispatcher. When the co-pilot receives the signal, he reports it to Harris.

Then the propeller on one of the engines begins to turn. The propeller is the fan-like part which turns very fast and makes the plane go through the air. The three blades of the propeller whirl faster and faster.

Now the pilot starts the other engine of the plane. He looks at the instruments to see that the engines are working all right. In front of the pilot there is an instrument board. But it has many more instruments than you would see in front of the driver of an automobile. The pilot uses these instruments in running and guiding his plane.

Harris nods to Smith, who then signals to the dispatcher. The great ship begins to move forward along the wet runway.

Even though it is getting dark, the pilots can see the field clearly. Lights show where the edges of the field are. White lights mark the runways. There are lights at the end of the runway. A light in a tower turns and turns. This beacon throws a beam of light out into the night and guides pilots to the field. They can see the beacon many miles away.

Both Harris and Smith are wearing head phones. Through these phones, they hear radio messages from airport control towers and weather stations. The men can also send messages by radio telephone.

Before Harris and Smith started their trip, the dispatcher gave them reports which came in about the weather all along the way. Weather reports are sent in every hour to the weather bureau at the airport, and the dispatcher gets them from the bureau. Sometimes the reports show that the weather is stormy along the route. Then the pilots try to choose a route which is not stormy.

United Air Lines

In an airport control tower men hear the radio reports from the planes. When one of these men hears from a pilot, he marks down where the plane is at that time. These men also hear about the weather from stations along the way. The control tower is a very busy place.

They have a plan for their flight which shows how high above the ground they should be at every point of the trip. It also shows the time at which they should reach each point.

The plane turns around at the end of the runway and stands ready to take off.

Harris tests his engines again Then he speaks through his microphone to the airport control tower and asks for his final instructions.

A man who works in the tower answers him. Harris speeds up his engines and starts down the long runway. Faster and faster goes the plane, and finally it lifts off the ground. It is in the air.

Before long the huge ship is in the clouds. The pilots cannot see the land below. They climb higher and higher through the clouds and rain.

Radio signals which come through Harris' head phones tell him that his plane is on its course. Even though the night is black and rainy and he cannot see, he knows he is on the right route. He obeys the laws of flying as men obey traffic laws when they drive automobiles.

Higher and higher the plane climbs.

American Airlines, Inc.

This plane is up above the clouds.

Then it comes out above the clouds. There are thin white puffy clouds, and the moon shines on them.

Up above the clouds the weather is better. The winds are blowing in the direction in which the plane is going. Harris grins at Smith. When they made their flight plan, they knew it would be safe to fly above the clouds. Now they have found good weather at this height.

Every half hour Harris hears radio reports of weather conditions along this route. During the night he knows what part of the country the plane is flying over. He knows how long it will take him to reach the next stop. He keeps his eyes on his instruments.

The men take turns flying the plane. The pilot of a passenger plane is not allowed to fly more than eight hours a day on this route. In the morning two other pilots are in the cockpit. Myers is flying the plane when it nears Los Angeles.

He calls to the airport control tower and says, "Los Angeles Tower, Trip 10, in range." The operator tells Myers which runway to use. He also says that the wind is blowing southwest at ten miles an hour and that several small planes are flying near by.

Myers circles and comes down through the clouds toward the field. There is the airport below in the bright daylight. The landing wheels touch the runway. The plane has reached the end of its journey.

A pilot such as Harris or Smith or Myers must keep well and strong. It would not be safe to ride in a plane if the pilot were not a healthy man. He must see his doctor often to be sure he is in good condition.

A pilot must study hard and take flying tests. Before a man becomes a pilot, he must fly many hours alone. He also must learn all he can about planes. He has to work hard on the ground before he is allowed to work in the air.

The Radio Man

Jim Burns works in the flight control tower of an airport. He is a radio man and does not wear a uniform as pilots do.

American Airlines, Inc.

This flight control tower is beside an airfield. There are big glass windows on all sides of the tower. Above is a light to guide the pilots who want to land on the field. The two men in the tower tell pilots when to take off and to land. When a plane does not have a radio, the men signal to it with the big light which you see inside the tower. This signal light shows two colors, green and red.

60

He sends messages out to the pilots who are flying to this airport. He tells them when the field is clear so that they can land. He tells them what to do when the weather is so bad that they cannot land.

This morning it is nearly time for a passenger plane to land at the airport where Burns works. Suddenly a heavy fog comes down over the field. It is hard to see even a little way. The fog is so thick that not even the lights around the edge of the landing field can be seen. Burns knows that it is dangerous for the pilot to try to land.

The pilot radios from his plane, "Jones speaking. United plane fifteen. Fog ahead. O. K. to come in?"

"Don't let down. Heavy fog here," Burns answers the pilot. Burns tells the pilot to fly the plane to the next city on the route.

Jones, high up in the sky, is battling strong winds. He would like to fly to the next city, but he does not have enough gasoline. He has to land soon. What shall he do? He cannot come down on a field covered with thick fog. He might crash into some building.

Again the pilot calls to the radio man and tells him the gasoline is nearly gone.

Jim Burns has already had reports from the other airports near the city. He knows they also are covered with fog.

So he calls an Army field on the other side of a low mountain. "Is your field clear of fog?" he asks.

"Yes," comes the answer.

Then Jim Burns speaks over the radio again and tells the pilot to land on the Army field. He also tells the pilot of the things which he must watch out for as he makes a landing at that field.

A few minutes later the plane comes down on the Army field. The pilot and his friends are safe. When Jones telephones his own field to tell of his arrival, he sends a message to the radio man in the control tower.

"Thanks, Burns. I couldn't have kept the engines going many minutes longer."

"Glad you got down safely, Jones. That's what a radio man likes to hear."

Caretaker of the Beacons

In the far western mountains an old man named John Edwards lives in a small cottage all by himself. He is hired by an airplane company to care for the beacon lights on the top of a mountain near by. As you know, beacons are signal lights which can be seen by fliers a long way off. Strong, bright beacons are placed high on towers, where they turn and turn as they send their beams out into the night. We say that they revolve on the towers. Where Edwards lives, the beacons are about ten miles apart.

In summer the old caretaker often sits on his doorstep watching the light as its beam flashes across the sky. He thinks of how this friendly light helps the pilots to keep on their route. The beacon shines out like the lighthouse beam to a sailor at sea. When a pilot sees a beacon, he knows that he is on a route which leads to a landing field.

The old man can turn the beacons on and off from his cottage. He turns them on at sundown and turns them off at sunrise. Some beacons turn themselves on and off, but not these which Edwards takes care of.

In each beacon there are two electric light bulbs. But the beacon uses only one of these bulbs at a time. The other is a spare, or extra, bulb like the spare tire on an automobile. When the bulb in use burns out, the other one lights up.

At times Edwards must climb the narrow trail that leads up the mountain to the beacon tower. At the foot of the tower is a little hut called the lighting plant. Inside this hut are the machines which light the beacon. Edwards must go inside and see that everything is in good order. If anything gets out of order, there may be no beacon light in the sky to guide the pilots. Then a pilot may get lost on his way. Of course, his radio will help him reach a landing field, but often he needs the beacon lights, too.

One snowy morning Edwards leaves his cottage to go up to the tower. As he steps outside, great snowflakes cover his cap and thick coat. The snowstorm is blinding.

He draws his coat tighter around him as he begins to fight his way up the mountain trail.

Big drifts of snow cover the trail. But the old man knows where the path ought to be. He has gone over this trail many, many times. So he pushes on a little way at a time. He stops now and then to rest because it is hard to climb in the deep snow.

Up the mountain path he climbs. Every time he puts his feet down in a snowdrift, it becomes harder to pull them out again. His legs grow stiff with cold. But old Edwards does not give up. He must reach the beacon.

After he has been climbing a long time, he pulls his big silver watch from an inside pocket. He is surprised to see that it is after four o'clock. It has taken him all day to reach the beacon tower.

Gray dusk is settling on the mountain. The beacon must soon begin its work.

As Edwards nears the beacon tower, he looks for the lighting plant. But the hut is nowhere to be seen. It is buried beneath the snow.

He pushes the snow aside to dig his way to the hut. With his arm he brushes the snow from the doorway. He opens the door and crawls inside. At once he drops to the floor and lies there breathing hard. His breath comes fast, puffing almost like a steam engine.

After a while, the old man raises himself from the floor. His breathing is quieter now. Soon he is able to walk about. Carefully he looks at all the machines and sees that they are in good shape to do their work. He can report that everything is in order.

Then he goes outside and looks up at the

beacon. It is revolving and throwing its light out through the darkness. The storm is not so bad now. It has stopped snowing, but the wind is still blowing. Edwards finds his tracks in the snow and slowly starts home.

The airway or route on which Edwards works is only one of the many airways over our country. Airways are the routes over which the pilots usually travel. Along the airways there are landing fields at which a pilot can land if his plane is not working right. Caretakers must take care of the lights around the landing fields as well as the beacon lights.

Many other men have special jobs to do to keep planes flying safely. Many women, too, work for the airways. The pilot, as you know, runs the plane. But the men who care for the beacons are helping the pilot to do his job. Men must work in the flight control room. Men must repair the planes and keep them in good order. Many men and women must do their jobs well if the pilot is to carry passengers safely across our country.

Mail and Express by Air

Ann Ames has just written a letter to her grandfather to wish him a happy birthday. " I wish I had sent him a letter or a card before this. This won't get there in time for his birthday."

" Then we'll send it air mail," says Ann's mother, " and he will get it tomorrow morning." She takes an air-mail stamp from a drawer in her desk and puts it on the letter.

An air-mail stamp shows that a letter is to go by air. Sometimes people use envelopes which have a red, white, and blue border and the words Air Mail printed on

The sacks in this picture hold mail which is being loaded into a
front cargo pit.

them.   It takes eight cents to send an air-
mail letter unless the letter is heavy.
Then it takes more.

Not long before, Ann and her mother
visited an airport and saw the mail trucks
bringing bags of mail to be loaded into

the cargo pits of the passenger planes. She saw passengers get on the planes in which the mail had been stored. So Ann knows how an air-mail letter travels.

" Mother, there won't be time to send Grandfather a present, will there? "

" Yes, if we send it by air express. Let's send him three jars of jam. He likes jam and has nobody at home to make it for him. You may pick out the kinds he likes best."

Every summer Mrs. Ames makes jam from some of the fruit which grows in her back yard. Jars and jars of fruit stand on the shelves of her big fruit closet in the basement.

Ann goes down the basement stairs. She stands and looks at the fruit on the shelves. Some jars are filled with cherries in sirup, and others have halves of peaches or pears in sirup. Other jars are full of

A man from the express company brings express packages to the men who load a plane. What parts of the plane can you see in this picture?

jellies, dark red, light red, or a deep golden. But Ann turns to the jars of jam. She knows that Grandfather likes jam best of all.

After looking at all the jars of jam, Ann chooses raspberry, strawberry, and blackberry. Then she carries the jars up to the kitchen table.

Ann and her mother wrap them in white tissue paper and tie a ribbon around each

72

one. There is a pretty birthday card to go in the package.

Then Mrs. Ames brings a shipping box and packs the jars of jam in it. She fills the empty spaces around the jars with packing material. Ann puts the birthday card in and watches while her mother closes the box. Mrs. Ames wraps it in thick paper and ties it with strong cord. Ann prints her grandfather's name and address neatly on the package. She writes her name and address in one corner.

Next Mrs. Ames telephones the Air Express Division of the Railway Express Company and says that she wants to send a package by air to St. Louis.

That afternoon a man comes to the house in an express truck. He weighs the package and tells Mrs. Ames how much it will cost to send the package by air express. Then he makes out an order showing where the package is to go and who is sending it. He gives Mrs. Ames a copy of the order, and she pays him.

After the expressman has called for other packages, he drives to the airport. The packages are put aboard the plane.

When the package reaches St. Louis, it is delivered to the house where Ann's grandfather lives. If it had gone by regular express, it would have taken two whole days longer. Air is the fastest way for passengers, mail, and express to travel.

Questions to Talk Over

1. Why do business men and women often travel by plane?
2. Would you enjoy taking an airplane trip across the country? Give reasons for your answer.
3. What kind of men make good pilots?
4. How does the radio man at the airport help the pilot?
5. What kind of worker was old John Edwards? Show that you are right.
6. Why do people send mail and express by air?

THINGS TO DO

1. Make a list of all the kinds of work you know which must be done if our passenger planes are to run. Be ready to tell which worker does each kind of work.

2. Fill a scrapbook with pictures showing planes which carry passengers, mail, and express. You can find many good pictures in newspapers and magazines. Cut out the pictures and lay them on the pages the way they will look best. Then paste the pictures neatly in the book. Under each picture write one sentence to explain that picture. Choose a title for your scrapbook.

3. Visit an airport to see planes land and take off. Watch to see passengers going aboard the plane. Notice the men and women who work on the planes and in the airport. See if you can tell what work each person does and what that person is called.

WORDS TO EXPLAIN

co-pilot	control tower	propeller
stewardess	flight plan	cargo pit
dispatcher	airway	galley
airport	beacon	seat belt
runway	fuselage	air mail
berth	cockpit	air express

J. B. Guss from Black Star

See this picture which was taken from a plane. Where do you see fields ready for planting? Find as many farmhouses as you can.

76

CHAPTER III

TAKING PICTURES FROM THE AIR

Making Maps of Our Farm Lands

"What a bright, sunshiny day to take pictures," says Hal Dale when he reaches the airport just before noon. He is speaking to Frank Stevens, who is a pilot.

"Not a cloud in the sky," Frank says. "Clouds are pretty in a picture, but they make shadows on the land."

Hal is a photographer. He makes his living by taking pictures and selling them. Today he is carrying a big camera, which he puts into place in the bottom of the plane. Next he moves several parts of the camera so that it will be ready to take the pictures. We say he sets the camera, just as someone might set a clock. Hal knows just how the camera ought to be set for the speed of Frank's plane. Hal looks the camera over to see that it is ready to use.

Frank climbs into the cockpit and turns to speak to Hal, who is in the cabin of the plane near his camera.

"You haven't left your film at home, have you?" Frank calls out.

Hal laughs. "Not this time. I'm sure I put it in the camera before I started."

Frank likes to joke with Hal about forgetting to put the film in the camera. Of course, Hal could not make pictures without film.

Before long the two men are high up in the air. In the cockpit Frank keeps his eyes on his instrument board. The plane climbs steadily higher and higher. The men can see farmhouses and roads far below them.

Now the plane is eighteen thousand feet above the earth. That is more than three miles. It is much farther than the distance most boys and girls go to school.

The pilot turns in his seat and calls to Hal, "The air is thin up here. We'd better put on our masks." Frank reaches for his mask. This mask is different from the one a smoke jumper wears. It is made of rubber and fits over Frank's nose and mouth.

Hal nods his head and reaches for his mask.

As anyone goes up very high into the air, he begins to feel that he cannot get enough breath. It has less oxygen than we need. If there is not enough oxygen in the air, some people get sleepy. Other people feel excited and sometimes even get silly when they do not have enough oxygen. Since Hal and Frank have work to do, they do not want to get sleepy,

Press Association, Inc.

This man is wearing the kind of mask which Frank and Hal wore. Over what part of the man's face does the mask fit? How does he keep it on? What is the tube for?

and they do not want to get silly, either.

The masks which Hal and Frank wear have tubes that go to a tank which holds oxygen. Now they turn the oxygen on and breathe through the tubes.

The plane climbs still higher. Then it stops climbing and flies forward. As it makes a wide circle high above the earth, Hal looks down at the land far below. The men want to be sure that they are above the land where Hal is going to take pictures.

The pilot looks down at the earth to be sure that he is above the right farm land. Again he circles over the land. Then he raises his hand. When he moves his hand down, Hal will know it is time to begin his work.

Hal sits with his hands on his big camera, which is in the floor of the plane. With this camera he can take pictures of the land below the plane. The lens of the camera is pointed down through an opening in the floor of the plane.

The lens is made of curved pieces of glass. When light goes through the lens,

Here is a photographer pointing the lens of his camera from the nose of a plane.

it makes a picture on the film. If you have had your picture taken, the part of the camera which was pointed at you was the lens.

As Hal watches, Frank moves his hand down. At once Hal presses some buttons on his camera, and it begins to click. Then Hal knows that the camera is taking pictures. At each click a little door is opened to let light go through the lens and take a picture. The camera takes one picture right after another while the plane flies over the land.

In the meantime Frank keeps looking at his instrument board. He watches the ground below. He must fly straight ahead over the ground where Hal wants to take pictures. He must not fly too fast or too slow. Frank knows that he must keep the plane at the same height from the ground as he goes back and forth. If the plane rolls to one side, the pictures will not be good.

Every little while Frank looks at a map which shows the ground that he must fly over. It shows many roads and rivers and towns. When Frank looks at it, he sees some of the roads which are on the ground below him. A line drawn on the map

Harold W. Kulick

This pilot who is standing on the ground has just landed after a trip in the plane to take pictures. There are five cameras in the nose of this plane. How many of them can you see?

shows the land that Hal wants to photograph. Other lines show the route which
the plane must take. Frank tries to keep
his plane on this route.

After a while Frank turns the plane
and flies back in the other direction. Hal
takes pictures of this strip of land as the
plane flies over it. Then as the plane flies
the other way again. he takes pictures of
the land right next to that strip. His
strips of pictures overlap each other. If
you have watched someone cut grass in a
yard, you know that he cuts one strip at
a time. You know, too, how the next strip
overlaps the first.

When all the pictures have been taken,
Hal says, " Now let's hurry home. I want
to see if I got good pictures."

" Fine," says Frank. Then the men fly
back to the airport.

After they land, Hal takes the big

Frederic Lewis

At the end of this table some pictures have been laid in place to make a map. See how each picture overlaps the next. In the middle of the table there is a map which is already finished. The pictures with white borders will be trimmed and made into other strips of the map.

camera out of the plane. " So long," he says as he gets into his car and drives off.

Hal goes to a darkroom and takes the film out of the camera. For a while he must work in the dark to make pictures from the film. If any light reaches the film, it will spoil the pictures.

Strips of pictures are made from Hal's film. Since Hal took the pictures from high up in the air, they show the farm lands from far off. The strips are overlapped to make a big photograph of the country over which the men flew.

This big photograph is really a map. It shows long roads, winding streams, and dark clumps of trees. It shows where one field ends and the next one begins. It shows pasture land for cattle, and lakes and ponds. The houses look like tiny squares on the map. A few fences show as shadows on the map. But they are short shadows because the sun was high in the sky when the pictures were taken.

Maps such as that made from Hal's photographs show quickly what the land is like. It would take a long time to walk over the ground and learn everything about it which the photographs show. Men who work for our government can tell from the map exactly how large the farms and fields are. They can tell how much food the farms will grow if the crops are good that year. Then they can tell whether our country will have as much food as it needs.

Pictures for the Bombardier

Hal's brother, Joe, is a photographer in the United States Army. Often Joe flies over enemy lands and takes pictures of what the soldiers are doing. He brings back pictures which our Army officers use in planning where bombs should be dropped.

This is one of our Army airfields as seen from the air. See if you can find some airplanes in the picture. Find two wide roads. What else do you see?

Today Joe must take pictures of an enemy town where airplanes are made. Around this town the enemy has many anti-aircraft guns to fire at planes in the air.

Joe has a very fast plane which carries plenty of gasoline. His plane does not carry bombs or guns to shoot down enemy planes. He has taken out of the plane everything which he does not need so that it will be as light as possible. If the plane were heavily loaded, Joe could not fly so fast. His plane is painted with a special paint so that you can hardly see it in the sunlight. Joe feels sure that if enemy planes see him today and try to follow him, he can fly fast enough to get away from them.

The day is clear and sunny, with big white clouds moving slowly in the sky. Joe knows he will be able to take good pictures, for the sun is so bright. He flies high above the ground. He flies so high that he must wear his oxygen mask.

As Joe flies, he looks often at his instrument board and down at a map which shows the land he must fly over to reach the enemy. He watches other instruments to see whether the wind is blowing hard enough to make his plane fly a little to one side. He watches the big clouds, too, for enemy pilots like to hide behind them and fly down to take him by surprise.

He looks back to see whether his plane is leaving a trail behind it in the air. Sometimes, if a plane gets up very high above the ground, tiny bits of ice form in the cold air as the plane passes through it. They make a trail which looks like smoke but is called a vapor trail. Then if enemy planes are near, their pilots can see the trail and fly to attack the plane. Joe wants to be sure that he is not leaving a vapor trail.

As he comes near to the town, Joe goes down a little lower. But he does not have to go close to the ground, for his camera takes good pictures at a great distance.

Now Joe presses a button, and his

The camera in this picture looks like a gun. Through what part of the camera does the photographer look before he begins to take pictures?

camera begins to click. He flies so fast that his plane seems to streak across the sky. His camera is a high-speed one, and he has set it to take pictures while the plane flies fast. Soon he has the pictures that the Americans need.

Just as Joe is ready to fly back to camp, he catches sight of an enemy plane rising from an airfield. He is glad that he has already taken the pictures. At first he thinks that the men in the plane do not see him, but they circle up toward him. They start to climb high enough in the air to shoot at him, but they are too late. Joe speeds up his plane and gets away. He is out over the sea on his way back to camp.

Joe flies toward the American airfield. When he reaches it, he circles overhead until he gets the signal to come in. Then he glides down and lands.

No sooner has Joe touched the ground than Dan, another photographer, takes out the part of the camera which holds the film. Dan rushes off with this part to a building near the edge of the field. In this building is a darkroom where pictures are made. They can be made right in a plane if it has a darkroom.

Joe's pictures are ready in a few minutes. Soon Joe is looking at them.

" You got good ones today," says Dan.

" They ought to be good," says Joe. " The enemy didn't see me until I was ready to start home. If I'd had bombs, I could have dropped them all over the town."

"Better leave that job for the bombardiers," says Dan. " They will be glad to see these pictures." A bombardier is the man whose job it is to drop bombs.

The pictures are large and clear. They show factories where the enemy makes airplanes. Railroads lead to these factories. The pictures show big tanks where oil is stored near the railroad tracks. Tank cars carry the oil to other places in the enemy's country. The pictures also show roads which lead out from the town.

Some pictures taken from a plane flying over enemy land have just been brought in. The officer who is seated looks through magnifying glasses at a picture. The other officer is pointing to the place where the pictures were taken.

Dan and Joe take the pictures to the American officers, who study them.

"The enemy must have been asleep while you took these pictures," says one of the officers as he looks at Joe's photographs. "They are the best I've seen."

"You were right over the center of

the town, Joe," says another. "Our bombardiers will know just what to do when they get there."

"When our bombs hit those airplane factories, the enemy planes will fly even if they don't have engines in them. They'll fly to pieces," says one officer.

Then Joe's pictures are studied by the American aviators who plan to bomb the town. Most of these aviators have never flown over this town before. Joe's pictures show them what it looks like from the air. They ask Joe questions about the route to take. They will try to drop their bombs on the railroads, factories, and oil tanks.

After the bombing is over, the officers want to know what damage the bombs did. They call Joe in and tell him to go back and take pictures of the town as it looks now. Joe gets into his plane and goes off to make photographs of the town again.

Joe knows that enemy planes will be waiting for him when he flies over the town this morning. It will not be so easy as the first trip. The enemy does not want the town photographed, for the Americans would then know how many of the factories were blown up or burned.

In an hour Joe's plane is coming near the town. He flies around very high in the air while he watches for enemy planes. They might see him and come up to meet him. Since Joe cannot fight back, he knows that he must take his pictures and get away in a hurry.

Then Joe goes down fast until he is over the place where the oil tanks used to be. He straightens out in order to take pictures. The enemy gunners see his plane, and Joe has time for only a few pictures. The anti-aircraft guns fire at him. But he gets away so fast that not a plane tries to follow him.

Joe makes a big circle and then flies back from a different direction. He takes more pictures of the town until he has used up all his film.

As Joe starts for home, he notices that big clouds are drifting along in the sky. He knows that enemy planes might be flying above the clouds, waiting for him. He keeps watching as he comes nearer to the clouds.

Then suddenly he hears the rattle of bullets hitting his plane. Straight ahead he sees a big cloud and flies into it. When he comes out into the sunlight again, the enemy plane is far behind him. His engines were not hit, and he gets home safely.

After Joe lands, he finds many bullet

holes in the wings of his plane. But his camera has not been hit.

When the officers study the pictures Joe has brought back this time, they see that the enemy's airplane factories have been blown up. Many buildings are partly burned. Not an oil tank is left. The railway cars have been thrown off their tracks. Until these cars are cleared away, no other trains can come into the town, and no trains can carry people out of the city. The railroad tracks have been torn up and will have to be built again.

Even though Joe took the pictures from high above the town, they show how much damage the bombs did. The bombardiers did good work against the enemy. But they could not have dropped the bombs in the right places if Joe had not brought back pictures of the town.

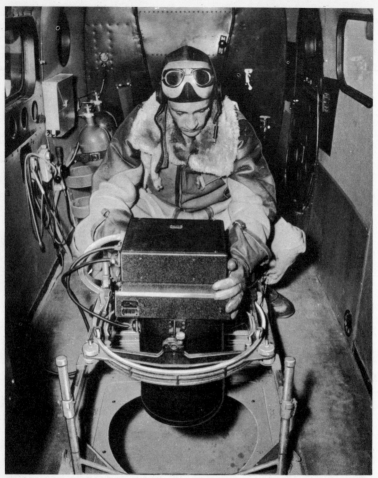

The photographer uses this camera to take air pictures at night. He uses flash bombs to light up the earth below. Where does this camera fit into the plane? Where is the lens of the camera?

100

Sometimes flying photographers travel in planes which carry machine guns. The photographer may take his pictures while the gunner is shooting at enemy planes.

Sometimes a photographer must take pictures at night. Because he needs light to take pictures, he takes along a special bomb which he drops over the place to be photographed. As it falls, it lights up the land. It is called a flash bomb. By the light of this flash bomb, Joe can get pictures at night which are almost as good as those he gets in the daytime.

If we did not have flying machines, we could not drop bombs on enemy land. If we did not have cameras which take pictures from a great distance, our flying photographers could not help us as much as they do. Their pictures help our men to learn about the enemy's country. Our men learn where the roads and bridges are. They learn where the enemy's soldiers are and where the big guns have been placed. The bombardier learns where his bombs should be dropped. He wants to drop them on the enemy's railroads, bridges, and factories. Other pictures help our men to learn what happened when the bombs fell on the enemy's land. Then the bombardiers know what to try to bomb on the next trip.

Photographing the Enemy's Camps

The sun is just beginning to rise in the east. This morning Joe is in a plane that is flying toward a city where enemy soldiers are camped. Today Joe is an observer. He does not have to fly the plane, for Fred Bowen, a pilot, is with him. From a great height Joe

Harold W. Kulick

This photographer is seated inside a bomber which is flying high above the ground. Where is his camera? Look at the things which he is wearing on his head. How many of them can you name?

looks down on the gray earth. As the morning light becomes clearer, he sees houses and roads in the country.

Today Joe has been sent out to take pictures of an enemy camp and to see what the enemy is doing. The American officers need to know whether the enemy has enough men and supplies to attack our soldiers.

As the plane comes near the city, Joe gets down near an opening in the floor of the plane. He holds strong field glasses to his eyes to see the ground below. The field glasses make it easy for him to see things that are far away from him. Then he writes down on a pad of paper what he sees. He works fast, for far below him he sees more signs of what the enemy is doing.

He sees railway yards with cars bringing supplies to the city. Trucks are coming in on the winding roads. It looks as if the enemy is bringing many soldiers and supplies to this place.

As the plane flies on, Joe presses certain buttons on his camera. He must have pictures of the scenes below. The camera begins to click.

Suddenly Fred swings the plane to one side. An enemy plane whizzes by, and Fred knows that bullets have hit the wings of his plane. Puffs of smoke are all around Fred's plane. The enemy gunners down on the ground are firing at the plane. They want to keep Fred and Joe from reaching home with pictures of the camp.

But still the cameras are clicking.

Then Fred sees fighter planes rising from below. These swift little planes try to cut him off before he flies out over the sea. But Fred's plane is so much higher in the air that he escapes before the enemy fighters can catch him.

Fred turns and grins at Joe as the plane races for the sea.

"We'll get back!" yells Joe. "Luck is with us."

Only a short time later Fred and Joe

U. S. Army Air Corps

These men have taken pictures from the air. They will go into the tent, which will keep out the daylight. Then they will take the film out of the camera and make pictures from the film. They must do this work in darkness. Sometimes a plane has a dark room where the men can work.

are back in the American camp. Joe tells the officers about the trains crowded in the railway yards and the trucks bringing supplies to the camp. He tells of the long lines of soldiers who were just arriving.

In a short time the photographs have been made, and the officers begin to study them. They can see that the enemy is almost ready to start a battle against the Americans.

"There's only one thing to do," says an officer. "We must fight them before they can move against us. Joe, these pictures you took today mean that we'll take the enemy by surprise."

Quickly the officers lay their plans. American airmen on other fields are told to be ready.

Soon planes are in the air. They rise from the field one after the other and fly toward the enemy camp. The great bombers fly steadily along. Above them fly the fighter planes to keep enemy planes from diving down to attack the bombers. On the sides there are other planes which can fly very fast. The air

107

is filled with the roar of the engines. The Americans are off to begin the attack before the enemy is ready!

Taking Other Pictures from the Air

Some of the stories which you have read here have told you a few reasons why we take pictures from the air. Such pictures are often used in making maps, as Hal's pictures were. Many strips of pictures are overlapped in making a map.

Sometimes a map is made to show parts of a big city where men are talking about putting up new buildings. Such a map shows the streets leading to the place. Then the men know whether that part of the city is too crowded to have more people come there to live or to work. They can even count the number of buildings already in any part of the city. Then they can choose the best places to build new streets. The men can also choose good places to put up buildings, like public libraries, which everyone uses. They want such buildings to be where people can reach them easily. They can also tell the best places to build more factories, more stores, and more houses for people to live in as the city grows bigger.

Maps are also made from air pictures when men need to build new roads from one place to another. From the maps men can see all the places where the roads might be built. A map will help them to find out how much it would cost to build a road over each route. They can tell where bridges would need to be built across streams. After studying a map made from the air pictures, men can choose the best route for a road.

A river has flooded this land. The river is shown in the front part of the picture. How high up on the houses does the water go? Do you see any land in this picture which is so high that the water has not reached it?

In time of flood, photographers take pictures from the air to show how far the water is spreading over the land. By studying the pictures, men can tell where to build walls which will hold the water back and keep the rivers from running over the land. Of course, photographers like to take pictures on bright days. But, if there is a big flood, they will take pictures even if the weather is not good. Their pictures may help rescuers to save many lives.

Sometimes when men want to know what kinds of trees grow in a huge forest, they have a photographer take pictures from the air. They study the pictures to find out whether there are many trees of each kind in the forest. They can even tell from the pictures about how much lumber, or wood, can be cut from the trees. They can tell from the hills and valleys in the picture where to build roads into the forest so that the trees or lumber can be brought out. Then they plan how to use the trees.

Perhaps you have seen air photographs in newspapers and magazines. If we had no airplanes or no men who knew how to use a camera in a plane, we could not have such pictures. We would not know how a wide view of our land really looks.

QUESTIONS TO TALK OVER

1. Why are photographs taken from the air? See whether you can find more reasons than those given in this book.
2. What kind of weather is best for taking air pictures?
3. How must a pilot fly a plane so that pictures can be taken to make a map?
4. Which would you rather be, a pilot or an observer in a war plane? Give reasons for your answer.
5. Why are airplanes sometimes called the eyes of the Army and Navy?
6. When does a photographer use a flash bomb?

THINGS TO DO

1. Gather all the air photographs which you can find. See if you can tell by looking at them why they were taken.
2. Make a drawing to show Joe's plane escaping from the enemy on his trip before the bombing.

3. Draw two pictures, one to show the enemy's railroad yard before it is bombed, and the other to show the same yard afterward.

4. Look at all the pictures you can find and pick out those which have been taken from a plane. Write a paragraph to explain how air pictures look.

WORDS TO EXPLAIN

air photographer   film
gunner   lens
bombardier   oxygen mask
anti-aircraft gun   flash bomb
high-speed camera   map
field glasses   vapor trail

See this big airship on an open field. Two men high up on a
pole, or mast, are tying the airship to keep it from rising up into
the air. Below the big bag is the car in which the crew ride.
Many airships like this one are kept in large buildings called
hangars.

CHAPTER IV

FIGHTING OVER THE SEA

Patrolling for Submarines

The sun has not yet come up, but at an airfield men are already busy. They are getting a big silver balloon ready to leave the field. Food is carried to the balloon from a truck. This balloon, or airship, is not an airplane, but it is used to do some kinds of work from the air.

The balloon is filled with a gas that is lighter than air. If the gas is let out of the balloon, the bag will fold up as a toy balloon does. The gas which fills the balloon is called helium. Helium is a very light gas which will not burn. Almost all the helium that we know about in the world today is in the

United States. Other gases are not so good for filling the bag of an airship. Some gases are not light enough, and some catch fire too easily.

Below the bag of the airship is the car in which the crew ride. It is like the body of an airplane. Frank Harvey gets into this car and takes the pilot's seat on the left. A second pilot takes the seat on the right. Instrument boards are in front of the pilots. The crew enter the airship and get into their places. This kind of airship is called a blimp.

Frank Harvey has orders to patrol the seas near some cities on our eastern coast. There are enemy submarines in these waters, waiting to sink American ships.

Submarines can travel under the water or on top of the water. When they are under the water, men on ships cannot see them. But from a blimp up above, the men can sometimes see the shadow of a submarine in the water.

Frank's blimp must watch over several American ships which are traveling together. These ships, which are bringing goods north, are called cargo, or merchant, ships. All the ships together are called a convoy. The blimp will stay near the convoy until the ships reach the end of their journey.

Inside the car of the blimp are seats for the men, and three beds called bunks. These bunks can be let down from the wall. The car is roomy and comfortable. All around are windows from which the crew can look out over the sea. On this trip they will look for submarines.

The blimp has two engines. But if

the pilot should stop the engines, the blimp would not fall into the ocean. The blimp would keep moving along because it is not so heavy as the air. We say that an airship is lighter than air but that an airplane is heavier than air.

A man on the ground calls to the men in the blimp, " Up ship! "

There is a strong wind blowing. At the signal the pilot starts his engines, and some men on the ground begin to let loose the ropes which hold the ship. The blimp rises into the air. If the wind were not so strong today, the blimp would have taxied around the field on its wheel before climbing into the air.

By the time the blimp is out over the sea, the sun has come up. Frank and his crew are soon above the merchant ships which they must protect from submarines.

Here is a blimp watching over a convoy late in the evening.
How many ships do you see in this convoy?

When the blimp reaches the ships, it
slows down. A blimp can travel much
faster than an ocean ship. Also it can
stay still in the air. It can move along
close to the water. So you see why a
blimp is good for patrol work.

While the blimp circles above the convoy, the men begin their watch for

This man who rides in the car of a blimp is looking for submarines. He is wearing a life jacket, which will keep him from sinking if the blimp should be shot down.

submarines. Through strong glasses they look down at the ocean. The water is moving in waves. The men look for oil on the water and for lines of bubbles. Oil or bubbles usually mean that a submarine is moving along under the water. With their glasses the men can sometimes see a submarine below the surface of the water.

After an hour or two one of the radio men begins to rub his eyes. He cannot bear to look at the water any longer. He can no longer see clearly.

Frank sees how tired the man is and says, " Jim, it's time for you to rest."

Jim is glad to stop his work. He pulls down a bunk, stretches out, and goes to sleep.

One or two of the men rest at a time. Even if they do not sleep, they stretch out comfortably and close their eyes.

The blimp seems to sail along in the air. Sometimes it seems to climb up a hill of air and to go down the hill on the other side. Sometimes the nose of the blimp is up and the tail down. But at other times the tail is up. The men hold to parts of the ship when the blimp is

121

tossed about in the wind. But they keep watching for submarines even when the air is rough.

The crew know that submarines try to keep under water during the day. If the blimp does not see the submarines and sink them, they may sink American ships.

Hour after hour the men watch the surface of the water. They take turns resting their eyes. As Jim looks through his glasses, he sees a dark shadow under the water right below the blimp. Then a black pole rises a little way out of the water. This black pole is the periscope of a submarine. When the periscope comes out of the water, the man in the submarine who looks through it can see if any ships are close by. If he sees ships, the submarine will stay below the surface. But the blimp is hard for him to see, for it is almost over his head.

Here the periscopes of a submarine are showing above the water. See the foam the periscopes make in the water. Some submarines have one periscope, and others have two.

Jim calls out to the captain, " There's a sub right below us."

The blimp goes down closer to the water. It stands still in the air over the spot while several men gather and look through their glasses.

Quickly some of the men swing open

the bomb bay, which is below the floor of the car. The bomb bay is the part of an airship or plane where bombs are kept.

The men in the blimp know how to drop bombs so that they will blow up a submarine. Down go two bombs. Then the pilot runs the engines fast, and the blimp moves away before the bombs hit the submarine.

There is a great roar, and two fountains of water gush up from the sea where the bombs strike. Then the water falls back into the ocean with a loud crash.

" There's the periscope again," cries one man of the crew. " The sub has had to come to the surface."

" Maybe the bombs didn't hit it, but they crushed its sides."

The men watch while the submarine rolls in the waves and goes under. It sinks never to come up again.

The men know that another submarine is probably close by. Several enemy submarines often travel together so that they can sink many ships. While the blimp circles over the convoy, the men watch carefully for another periscope.

In the meantime the ships which the blimp is protecting have moved on their way. Frank circles around them again and again, and his men look for more submarines.

If the blimp did not bomb the submarine, some of the merchant ships might be sunk, and the men on the ships might be lost. The goods which the ships are bringing to us would never reach our country. Sinking our merchant ships is one way which the enemy uses to fight us at sea. But this time a blimp has sunk a submarine and saved our ships.

Later that day Frank sees that one ship

in the convoy has fallen behind the others. He knows that this ship must be having trouble with its engines. Enemy submarines like to find a ship which is alone on the ocean. Frank flies the airship back so that his men can watch the waters around this ship.

In the late afternoon a periscope comes up out of the water where the setting sun makes a bright path on the ocean. Frank signals to one of the fast little destroyers that dart about the convoy. The destroyer goes to the spot where the periscope was seen. It drops bombs into the sea, and fountains of water rise high in the air. Pieces of the submarine come up to the surface, and oil spreads over the waves. But this time the men do not see the sinking submarine.

Today has been an exciting day for Frank and his men. On many trips the crew watch day after day without seeing a submarine.

Frank always keeps the blimp close to our coast. If a blimp needs to go to a part of the ocean where it may meet enemy planes, it must be protected by fighter planes. The bag of the blimp is so large that it could easily be hit by a gunner in a plane. Then the gas would leak out, and the blimp would sink.

On an Aircraft Carrier

In the darkness of the early morning a ship is moving far out at sea. Its top is a long deck, or floor, called the flight deck. This deck is so long that airplanes can land on it or take off from it. The ship is called an aircraft carrier because planes use it as they use an airport. It carries gasoline, bombs, and torpedoes for the planes.

Official U. S. Navy Photograph

These pilots are in a room on an aircraft carrier listening to their commander. Some of the men will take off in the dark. They wear dark goggles until they are ready to get into their planes. Then their eyes will be used to the dark when they fly. What else are the pilots wearing?

Below the deck of the carrier there are many rooms. In one of these rooms a group of airplane pilots listen to their commander. He has learned that an enemy force is near. The pilots are to fly their planes this morning in an attack on the enemy. The commander tells them

128

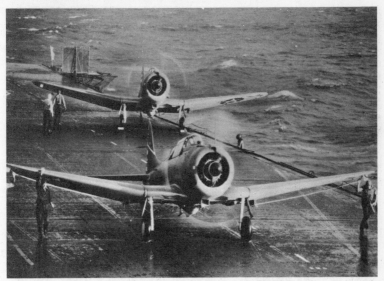

These dive bombers stand ready to take off from an aircraft carrier. The deck is wet and slippery, but the planes will do their work. Can you see the propellers? Why?

what to do after they take off from the carrier.

While the men sit quietly listening, a plane is brought up to the flight deck. The plane comes up on an elevator from a lower deck. Its wings are folded so that it does not take up too much space.

Official U. S. Navy Photograph

See how the planes are placed on the carrier's deck. To the left is the tower of the carrier. The tower is the part of the carrier where the smoke stacks are. The captain of the carrier and the lookouts work in the tower. It is at the edge of the carrier's deck so that the planes will have enough space to land and take off. On other ships the tower is in the middle of the deck instead of at the edge.

Now its wings are unfolded, and men push the plane into place on the flight deck.

Another airplane is brought up, and another, and another. Soon there are rows and rows of planes at one side of the deck all ready for their pilots.

Then down in the room where the pilots are listening, the order is given, " Man your planes."

The pilots rush up to the deck and climb quickly into their planes.

" Pilots, start your engines," comes the order over the loud speaker. There is a great roar as the pilots start their engines. The propellers whirl in the air. It is not yet daylight, but the men are eager to take off.

Standing by are the strong men of the flight-deck crew. They have special work to do with the planes. They wear cloth helmets of different colors. Those with the yellow helmets direct the pilots when they land and take off. Those with the blue helmets take charge of the planes when the pilots are not in them. There are also men on the carrier who wear red helmets. They repair the planes when they get out of order or come back with holes shot in them.

" Get ready to launch planes," comes the next order. The planes must take off one at a time. Each pilot waits until the signal is given him.

Dusty is the leader of the first squadron, or group, of fighter planes which will take off. He sits in his plane and watches a man in a yellow helmet. This man will signal Dusty when it is time for him to fly. The nine planes in Dusty's squadron are all ready to take off.

Another man in a yellow helmet holds up a flag. As Dusty looks, the man lets the flag down. At this signal Dusty starts his plane up the deck. It goes faster and faster and soon rises from the deck. It climbs into the dark sky and turns away from the carrier.

The other men in Dusty's squadron wait

for their signals. Each one takes off
when his turn comes. In a short time
they meet in three groups of three planes
each. When planes fly together in groups,
we say that they are flying in formation.

Many other planes leave the deck after
Dusty's squadron. The fighter planes always leave first. They go ahead of the
bombers to see whether enemy planes are
near.

Dusty and his fighters are on their way
to hunt for enemy planes and shoot them
down. Dusty's plane is a small, fast one.
It carries no bombs or torpedoes but has
two machine guns. They are fired from
the front of the plane. His plane can
climb very fast and can also dive quickly.
It can dive down close to a ship and then
dart high into the sky again. If the plane
carried bombs or torpedoes, it would be
too heavy to dart about.

As Dusty climbs and circles in the air, he looks carefully all around. There are big clouds in the sky, and it is getting light enough for him to see a long way. How he would like to use his guns on an enemy plane! But no enemy planes are in sight. He hears only the roar of his engines.

Dusty keeps on looking about. Suddenly he sees a large squadron of enemy scout bombers far below him. There are eighteen bombers in the squadron. They are flying in the direction of the American aircraft carrier.

If the bombers see the carrier, they will try to dive down over it and drop their bombs on it. The bombs might blow up the carrier, and all the planes still there would be lost. Then Dusty's plane and the other planes which have left the carrier would have no place to go when their

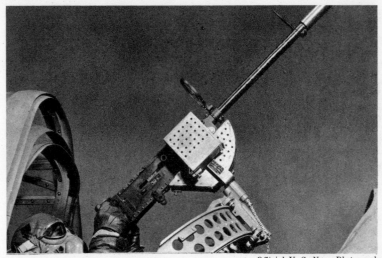

Official U. S. Navy Photograph

This man is a gunner in a dive bomber. He can turn his gun in different directions to hit enemy planes. What part of the gun does he look through when he aims? Why is he wearing gloves?

gasoline is used up. They would have to come down at sea, for there is no land near by.

Dusty also knows that an enemy bomber has machine guns at the front of the plane. At the back of the bomber there is also a gun which can be turned to point toward an enemy plane. The

135

man who rides in this part of the plane and fires this gun is called a tail gunner.

Dusty's plane is faster than the bomber. He races along toward the enemy but keeps high up in the air. The other pilots in his squadron follow. Next Dusty raises the nose of his plane and climbs. Maybe the bombers far below have not yet seen the fighter planes. Anyway Dusty wants to get his men high up among the clouds. Then they can dive down on the enemy. Perhaps Dusty can take the enemy by surprise. He wants to shoot the bombers down before they can see where the carrier is.

Then Dusty tips his plane to one side to signal his squadron that he is going to dive on the enemy. He dives down out of the clouds until he is behind the bombers. Then he flies straight toward the leader and fires his guns. Down goes the leader's plane out of the sky. But the other bombers close in and fly right on. Suddenly Dusty feels enemy shells hit his plane. For a minute the plane shakes as if it may crash. But the engine is still working, and Dusty goes on.

As Dusty circles away, one of his men comes down toward the bombers with his finger on the firing button, or trigger. His guns are shooting as he darts past, and one bomber bursts into flames. A moment later it tumbles down and makes a big splash as it hits the water below.

Now Dusty sees another plane in flames. This time it is an American fighter. Dusty hopes that the pilot will be able to use his parachute and jump from the plane in time. But as the plane falls, he sees no sign of the pilot.

Dusty shoots at another plane. But this time he misses. The bullets whiz by the side of the enemy plane. As Dusty watches, he sees several other enemy bombers scattering, with American fighter planes after them.

Then Dusty comes in on the remaining bombers from behind. He waits to shoot until he is close to them. One more enemy plane falls down toward the sea in a burst of smoke and fire, and another explodes like a firecracker. Dusty's bullets have hit the gas tank.

Before the other bombers can turn on him, Dusty circles up and comes back into them. His guns are firing. But this time they miss again, and a shell tears a hole in one of Dusty's wings.

The enemy bombers fly off in all directions. Dusty would like to follow and keep shooting at them, but his plane is too badly shot up.

When the enemy planes have gone,

Dusty signals his squadron to go back to the carrier. Though his plane has been hit many times, he himself is not hurt. But it is hard to guide the plane, for some of its parts have been shot away. Two of his men fly in formation near him, and the others follow. One plane has been lost, and the pilot of another signals that he is wounded. The squadron must return to the carrier, for some of the men have no bullets left and not much gasoline. They want to tell about the enemy bombers. Dusty and his men have not been fighting long, but they have saved the carrier.

The captain of the carrier is watching for the men to return. The crew turns the carrier so that the planes can land easily.

When Riley, the wounded pilot, lands, a man with a red cross on his helmet takes care of him. Riley is put in the sick bay, or hospital room, down in the carrier. Dusty visits him later. The doctor says that Riley must stay in bed for a week or so.

Soon other planes have landed on the deck, all but Morton's, which was shot down. After the captain hears about the enemy bombers, he orders his crew to move the carrier to another part of the ocean so that the enemy cannot find it easily.

A carrier is like an airfield for planes at sea. It is called a base, or a place where the pilots can return for gasoline and repairs. Planes often use an island as a base, but the island cannot move about as a carrier does. The enemy knows where the island is and can attack any planes that may be there.

The enemy's land may be so far away

Official U. S. Navy Photograph

Which ship in this picture is an aircraft carrier? How do you know? The planes are returning to the carrier. They are circling overhead and will land one at a time.

141

that our planes cannot fly there from a land base and get home again. An aircraft carrier can take its planes into the enemy's waters and launch its planes near the enemy. After our planes have done their work, they can return to the carrier in another part of the ocean. Sometimes a carrier goes to meet its planes.

A carrier has guns to fire at enemy ships. But it is not built to protect itself as a warship is. The carrier tries to get out of the way when it is attacked. Some of its planes stay on deck so that they can get into the air fast to protect the carrier from enemy planes.

Bombing Enemy Ships

No sooner have Dusty and his men landed on the carrier than a call is heard through the ship.

"Targets for bombs! Targets for bombs

at Tono!" A voice comes over the loud speaker. By target is meant something to shoot at or to bomb. A target may be an enemy ship or a carrier or troops landing. The leader of a bombing squadron tells his men that they are taking off on a flight to bomb what they find at Tono.

Dusty watches a minute before he goes below. The leader's bomber takes off first. And now another bomber flies away from the carrier. In a few minutes nine bombers are in the air heading west.

One bomber flies ahead of the others. Jack is the pilot in this plane. He has been hoping for a good target, and he cannot reach Tono soon enough.

It is a bright, sunny morning, and the ocean is very blue. The men can see a great distance ahead of them. They keep careful watch, but no enemy planes are in sight.

After a while Jack sees a wide sandy beach. The beach curves around until it almost makes a circle of water, or a bay. Inside the bay the water is still. An enemy ship is entering the bay from the ocean, and Jack knows that this is Tono.

He looks closely at the ships in the bay. One is a fast new warship. There are two rows of supply ships and three tankers which carry oil. A few submarines and other ships are at a pier, or platform built out into the bay as a landing place. There are several seaplanes floating in the bay. These are planes which can land on water and take off from it. There is a seaplane tender, a ship which takes supplies to the place where the seaplanes are.

As Jack and the other pilots speed over these targets, they see something else. On the wide beach are two huge airplanes. Jack flies a little lower to look at them.

144

He sees that each plane has four engines. But he must not stop to look at these planes.

It has been only a few minutes since Jack first saw Tono, but already the enemy ships have begun to shoot at the bombers up above. The bombers no longer stay together as the anti-aircraft guns turn on them. One of the warships has as many as thirty guns shooting. Jack and the other pilots know they must act quickly.

Jack puts the nose of his plane down and begins to make a steep dive. He has the bomb bay open. He aims at a huge warship which has an airplane on its deck. The gunner is ready for any fighter planes that may come up to meet the bombers.

As the bombs strike the ship, a big roar is heard. Flames shoot up into the sky. The men on the ship stop shooting at the planes. Jack has pulled out of his dive

Here are twin anti-aircraft guns on an American ship. Which men do you think shoot the guns? What might some of the other men do? If you look closely, you may see where the men keep shells for the guns. The part of the ship around the gun is called the gun nest.

and circles around to fly over the warship again.

One of the other planes drops a bomb on a submarine at the pier. It blows up and sinks. The plane circles and comes back to drop its last bomb. Then the pilot turns the plane toward the carrier and speeds home.

Fighting is going on all around Jack. Shells from the anti-aircraft guns burst in the air near him. Jack knows that these bursting shells can set his plane afire. Such shells go off like great firecrackers and leave puffs of smoke in the air.

Ahead of him, Jack sees an American plane that has been hit by a bursting shell. Smoke fills the air about it, and it drops down into the ocean. Jack wonders which of his friends have been lost. Then a shell bursts near his own plane, and pieces of it crash into his wings.

Jack has dropped his last bomb on a seaplane. Soon he is out over the water again, catching up with the pilots who have already left Tono. He heads back for the carrier. The crew look back at the curving beach and watch the clouds

This plane has just let a torpedo go. Soon the torpedo will enter the water and go very fast to its target. The plane is flying low over the water.

of smoke rising from the burning ships.

The men know that torpedo planes have been sent from the carrier. These planes are the largest on the carrier, but they cannot move so fast as the fighter planes. As Jack flies onward, he hopes that the torpedo planes will blow up the other warships in the bay.

This officer signals a plane to come aboard the carrier. He has a paddle in each hand. By moving the paddles about, he can give different messages to the pilot up in the plane. The pilot may have to stay in the air circling until the deck is clear.

When the bombers reach the carrier, they circle overhead until they can land. Then the signal is given for Jack to bring his plane aboard. His wheels touch the deck, and he taxies ahead. His plane must be out of the way before another pilot can land. Almost before Jack's plane comes to a stop, men rush out and roll it out of the way.

The deck crew work fast, and soon the eight bombers are safe in their places. The men find out which of their comrades have been lost.

Jack and his men are hungry after their sea fight. They go down into a room in the carrier to get coffee and sandwiches.

The wounded men are taken down to the sick bay. One pilot has been hit in the arm by pieces of a bursting shell. When his arm has been bandaged, he joins the others for some food.

As soon as the planes are loaded with gasoline and bombs, Jack will lead his men back to the fight. Several planes will need repairs, but other planes are ready to take their places.

" Did you see your bomb hit the war-ship? " one pilot asks another.

"Yes, it hit right on the bow." The bow is the front part of a ship.

"My first bomb went on through the deck and must have exploded below. How I wished for just one more bomb!"

Jack is quiet as he listens to the others. The boys have done a good job today.

Planes Help in Other Ways

Often our fighting on the seas is far away from home. Supplies have to be sent to our men so that they can keep on fighting. Big transport planes carrying heavy loads go back and forth from our country to distant places where the men fight.

Sometimes these giant planes carry cargo to a battle front. They are loaded with bombs, torpedoes, shells, airplane engines, airplane propellers, and some medicine for wounded men. They may carry tanks and small cars called jeeps. In three or four days a plane can reach a battleground on the other side of the world. If the supplies were sent by ship, it would take three or four weeks for them to get there.

Transport planes also carry soldiers and airmen to distant places. In some planes folding benches can be let down for the men to sit on. Sometimes there are no seats. Men sit on the cargo or on the floor. The planes do not have berths as some of our passenger planes have. Berths take up too much space.

When a transport plane returns to our country, it carries a heavy load. It may bring back wounded men, perhaps from an aircraft carrier. Or the transport plane coming from a far-off country may bring supplies which we need.

Here is a huge convoy carrying men and supplies to a distant battle front. Warships and seaplanes protect this convoy. You can see the wing of the photographer's plane in the picture.

As you know, planes also help to protect our ships. Sometimes seaplanes go with a convoy to a battle front. Large numbers of soldiers with their supplies travel on hundreds of transport ships. Warships also go along to protect this convoy and to serve as a base for the sea-planes. The planes look for enemy sub-marines, ships, and airplanes. Though the crew may watch many, many days, nothing exciting may happen. When planes are watching over a convoy, sub-marines usually stay out of sight.

Airplanes also do rescue work at sea. Sometimes a pilot has engine trouble and cannot keep up with the other planes in his formation. He may get lost in a fog. He may have to come down on the water when he has used up his gasoline. For a while his plane will float because of two large bags filled with gas, which are built into it. But after many hours holes come in the bags and let the water in. The pilot knows the plane will soon sink. Then he puts his rubber boat into the sea. He takes food and drinking water, gets into the

This flying ship has landed on the water to rescue the men in
the rubber life raft.

rubber boat, and leaves the sinking
plane. The pilot may float for days in
this boat before his friends find him.
The rubber boat is bright yellow in color
so that searching planes can see it
easily from the air. When a pilot in a
seaplane sees the yellow spot on the
water, he comes down close by.

155

Sometimes a pilot patrolling the ocean sees men floating on a raft. If he is flying a land plane, he cannot come down on the sea. But he drops food and water to the men and calls a ship to come to the rescue. Of course, seaplanes can land near a raft or lifeboat.

QUESTIONS TO TALK OVER

1. How do blimps help to patrol the seas in time of war?

2. Why do we sometimes use blimps rather than planes to patrol the seas near our coasts?

3. Would you like to work on a blimp? Give reasons for or against being one of the crew.

4. What happens on an aircraft carrier when the men get ready to attack the enemy?

5. Why do you think our country uses so many different kinds of planes?

THINGS TO DO

1. Make a booklet to show each kind of plane you know. Paste some pictures in the booklet or

draw pictures showing a fighter plane, a scout bomber, a patrol bomber, a torpedo bomber, a seaplane, and other kinds of planes. Under each picture write two or three sentences to tell what that plane can do.

2. Write a short paragraph to explain why we use aircraft carriers in fighting at sea.

3. Make a list of ways in which planes help us at sea. Begin your list like this:

Fighting the enemy.

Carrying supplies to our men in far-off places.

4. Watch the sky to see a group of planes flying in formation. Count the number of planes in the group. Draw a picture showing how the planes make up the flight formation.

Words to Explain

blimp	aircraft carrier	patrol
fighter plane	seaplane tender	convoy
scout or dive bomber	flight deck	submarine
patrol bomber	bomb bay	periscope
torpedo bomber	bunk	formation
transport plane	squadron	pier
seaplane	target	helium

Bombs are being loaded into this plane. See the open doors of the bomb-bay. The bombs are hung on racks above these doors.

Here is a heavy bomber plane. How many engines does it have?

CHAPTER V

FIGHTING OVER LAND

Bombing an Island from the Air

Far away from our country lies a large island used by the enemy. It is in the midst of a sea where many ships travel. On this island are rocky hills and mountains. There are towns and farms but not many trees. Along the coast are cities where ships can stop.

For many days our planes and those of our Allies have been bombing important places on this island. Our Allies are the countries which are fighting on our side in a war. This morning hundreds of planes are coming in over the island.

People on the island look up at the

sky as they go about their work. They see line after line of huge American bombers coming nearer. Most of the people rush to shelters to escape being hurt, but some stay to watch the planes.

For days the crews of these bombing planes have been studying photographs of the island. They have looked at maps which show the roads and airports and buildings used by the enemy. So they know where to drop their bombs. Each squadron of planes has orders to bomb certain targets.

The bombers roar over the railroad yards where many tracks come together. Enemy troops have been loading trains with supplies.

Up in the air a bombardier takes control of the plane. Then the cry comes, "Bomb bay open!"

Over the railroad yards, the bombardier

drops some of his bombs and calls out, "Bombs away!" His work is done, and the pilot takes control of the plane again.

As the bombs fall into the railroad yards, buildings are blown up. Great fires start as the railway station and cars catch fire. The supplies inside the cars begin to burn. Flames leap up toward the sky.

Enemy soldiers in the railroad yards run here and there as they hunt for shelter. Those who fire the anti-aircraft guns try to shoot down the American planes. Great clouds of smoke rise from the yards. If the trains are burned up, the soldiers cannot travel quickly from place to place on the island. There will be no way of sending supplies to the men in other camps.

Now the American planes turn to fly over another railway yard. A bomb hits an engine pulling some loaded cars.

Black smoke rushes high up into the air. The engine flies to pieces, and the cars are tossed to one side. Some of the cars are loaded with shells for big guns. When the cars begin to burn, the shells explode as if they were fired out of guns. The tracks are twisted, and there are deep holes in the roadbed. It will be a long time before trains can travel over this railroad.

Bombs fall on the barracks, or long houses, where enemy fliers and mechanics live. The barracks are blown to bits.

A rain of bombs comes down on an airfield. A big hangar which is filled with enemy planes catches fire. The tanks of the planes blow up. The Americans up in the sky are careful not to bomb the runways. They want to capture the island, and they try to save the runways for their planes. The Americans fly on to

This picture was taken while bombs were bursting on an enemy airfield. Bombs have fallen into the water near an enemy ship. Where do you see runways in the picture? Where are roads shown?

bomb other airfields on the island. They want to blow up every enemy plane they can find.

Several planes fly over the hotel where the enemy leaders do their work. Bombs hit the roof and fall inside. There is a loud explosion. Soon the hotel is on fire.

163

Near by is a building in which messages are sent by telephone or telegraph. This building crumbles in smoke and ruins. Nothing is left but smoking fires. Now the enemy cannot send news by telephone or telegraph from the island. The leaders cannot get news easily.

Still plane after plane comes over the island. It looks as if they will never stop. As some planes fly away to their base, others arrive in groups of three.

Anti-aircraft shells are bursting in the air, but the planes are so high that not many of the shells explode near them.

A few enemy planes go up to the fight. But they are met by small, swift fighter planes which have come along with the American bombers. These fighter planes dart about and drive off most of the enemy planes. Only a few American planes are shot down.

This gun is in the nose of the plane. The gunner will fire if enemy planes attack at the front of the plane.

The Americans are beginning a big battle by bombing many important cities and airfields. After these places are damaged or destroyed from the air, it will be much easier for American soldiers to fight on the ground and capture other places. The Americans and their Allies need to capture the whole island. They use airplanes to clear the way for their armies.

165

Landing Paratroopers

That night as soon as the sky is dark, many American transport planes head for the island. The planes skim along not far above the water. By flying low the pilots hope that enemy planes will not see them. Whitecaps from the strong wind show on the water.

Inside a plane two rows of young men sit facing each other. Some seem to be sleeping, but most of them are excited. They talk and laugh.

" Have you ever jumped under enemy fire? " one man asks another.

" No," answers the fellow sitting beside him, " but I've taken practice jumps in the dark many times."

" We'll soon know what it's like to parachute down into enemy country," says an officer.

The men wear helmets and jumping suits fastened with zippers. They have boots which reach nearly to their knees. They carry sharp knives, pistols, and Tommy guns, which are small machine guns. Every man is wearing a parachute and carries matches, food, drinking water, and a first-aid kit. The men have crossed water patrolled by enemy planes, but some of them have not yet fought against the enemy. They all want to land and do the part of the work that they have been taught to do.

Most of the jumpers on the planes are soldiers. But there are also a few others who are going on this trip to take care of the soldiers. Some of the jumpers are doctors who have medicines and other things which the soldiers may need.

For several days these men have known that they were going to parachute down into an enemy country. But they have not known what part of the enemy land it would be. Now each group has orders to capture certain important places on the island. When the men drop from the planes, they will try to land near these places. Then they may be able to surprise the enemy.

Soon the men see that land is ahead. They have crossed the water between their camp and the island.

Now the pilot begins to climb higher in the air. He must fly the plane up high enough above the land so that the parachute soldiers, or paratroopers, will have time to drop safely with their parachutes. Then they can see what part of the country they are landing in.

As the plane travels on, the air is rough. There are high winds tonight. It is not always safe to jump from a plane when

168

the wind is high. A strong wind may throw the jumper against the ground or swing him into trees. It may keep him from landing at the right place. But the men have no thought of putting off their trip. The battle is all planned. Other men will expect the paratroopers to do their work first. It is too late to change the plans for the big attack.

Now Mark Johnson, the co-pilot, comes into the cabin. He shouts, "We'll be over the dropping zone in fifteen minutes!" The dropping zone is the place where the jumpers will leave the plane. Usually the men call it the D. Z.

A few minutes later Mark comes again. "D. Z. in ten minutes," he says.

The leader signals the men to stand up and get ready. They jump to their feet and hook their parachutes to the wire over their heads. They form a line between the seats. The soldiers' suits are heavy, and their pockets are filled with the things that they must carry with them.

Now a light is turned on near the door. When the men see this light, they know that they must jump in four minutes.

They look out of the plane but can see little of the country. The moon is low in the sky. Fires burn here and there on the island. They were lighted by bombs which the Allies dropped during the day.

When the plane reaches the part of the island where the men are to jump, flares are thrown out. These flares do not light up right away. They burn a little later and light the way for the troops. They flare up for a few minutes and then go out.

After the flares are dropped, another light flashes on inside the plane. It is the go-ahead signal.

This American paratrooper has just jumped from his plane. Soon he will land among the trees below. See how the strip of cloth which holds his parachute is being unwrapped. This strip is fastened to the plane. As soon as he has fallen away from the plane, his parachute will open.

How many paratroopers have just jumped from these three
Army transport planes?

Out goes the first man in line. As he
jumps, he gives a loud shout. His parachute streams out behind him and opens
like an umbrella.

As the plane travels on, the men dive
out into the darkness one by one. Each
one shouts as he goes. The pilot watches
until the last man jumps. Then he turns
the plane toward the water.

As the first jumper holds on to the lines of his parachute, he looks around and then down at the ground. There is a grove of trees beneath him. He pulls the lines on his parachute to change his direction.

Enemy troops are watching from the ground. They turn on great searchlights to help find the planes. The lights sweep over the sky and make it as bright as day. Here the enemy sees a jumper on his way down. Then the light follows the big transport plane from which he jumped. The enemy fires anti-aircraft shells at the transport, but the plane is too far away for the shells to reach it.

Enemy soldiers are watching for paratroopers and try to reach the places where they may land. Before some of the men can get out of their parachutes, they are taken prisoner by the enemy.

Many paratroopers have been blown by

the wind away from the places where they wanted to land. They are scattered out over the island in the darkness. As they move about, they whistle signals to each other. When the signals are answered, they meet in small groups and go toward the places they must capture.

A group of ten men head toward an airfield. They know that enemy planes will be standing on the field and in the hangars. They hear a whistle and answer it. Soon they are joined by several other paratroopers who have been separated from their group.

Paul, their leader, goes ahead and begins his work. Soon planes and hangars are blazing. A few enemy guards run out onto the field, and there is sharp fighting. Some of the Americans are captured, and a few are wounded. But before long the field is captured by the Americans.

Paul sees some planes signaling from the air. With a flashlight he signals to them that the paratroopers have taken the airfield. In a short time planes of the Allies begin to land.

The troops which you have been reading about fight on the western side of the island. A little earlier some paratroopers of our Allies landed on the eastern side of the same island. To the enemy the island seems alive with paratroopers.

All over the island groups of paratroopers have been carrying out their orders. By morning they have captured many important airfields and towns on the coast. They take several ports, and American troops come in from ships. They bring supplies ashore without fear of the enemy.

The paratroopers have made it safe for soldiers to land on the beaches. Soon jeeps and tanks are rolling along the roads which the paratroopers have taken from the enemy. Because the battle was carefully planned, it seems certain that the island will soon be captured.

Mr. Grease Monkey

Next morning a big American transport plane comes to a captured airfield on the island. Men in wrinkled brown overalls step out. These mechanics, who call themselves " grease monkeys," will keep the American planes in good condition.

Every time a plane returns from a trip, these mechanics will test it and put every part in good working order. They will check the gas, the oil, and the tires. When a plane comes back with holes shot in it and its machinery damaged, these men will rebuild it if they can. They know how to do everything that needs to be done.

Official U. S. Army Air Forces

How many mechanics do you see in this picture? Some mechanics work on the engine. Other mechanics must keep the instruments, the radios, the propellers, and other parts in good working order.

Other men come to rebuild the hangars which were hit by shells.

Transport planes bring gasoline and oil for the planes to use until ships can bring more supplies. The Americans will need bombs and shells, too. The mechanics will need tools and new parts to put into the planes. And there must be food for all these men.

The mechanics have no guns to fight back at the enemy. But they are used to working in dangerous places. If enemy planes try to take the airfield again, the grease monkeys will keep working on the planes while our fighter planes go up to drive the enemy away.

Jay Robinson is one of the grease monkeys. As he steps from a plane, he quickly looks the field over. United States bombers and fighters are all about. Jay and three other mechanics head for a big bomber which has just landed. The bomber had been badly damaged by the enemy, and the pilot had to land. He could not fly the plane back to its base across the water.

Mark Johnson sees the mechanics and comes rushing out to meet them. Mark

See this fast mechanic at work on a plane. He has put in a new part and is fastening down the hood, or covering, of the engine. What other part of the plane do you see in the picture?

is the co-pilot of the plane which brought some of the paratroopers to the island the night before. The anti-aircraft gunners of the enemy had fired at him and struck one engine. The tail of the plane had been hit, too, and there were many bullet holes in the wings.

Jay, who is one of Mark's regular ground crew, looks the plane over and shakes his head. "Hard job the first thing when we land, but we'll try to get it together for you, Mark. Your Green Dragon will soon be flying again."

"But the Green Dragon needs a new engine. You grease monkeys can't make one out of nothing. I know there aren't any parts here," says Mark.

"We'll patch your Dragon up so that you can fly it back to the base," says Jay. "Maybe we'll find a good engine there in a plane that is badly wrecked. Put a good engine in and your plane will be as good as new. Those holes in the tail and wings can be patched up easily."

Near by is a high platform, built with steps so that the mechanics can climb up to work on the engines. Jay moves the platform over and begins work.

He starts an engine of the plane, but he does not like the sound of its roar. He and the other mechanics soon see that this engine needs many small parts. One of the blades of the propeller is bent. A machine gun in the back of the plane will not work.

" Don't see how Mark ever got back with this plane," says Jay.

" He probably just glided in," answers another mechanic as he keeps on with his work. " The mechanics back at the base will have the parts they need to repair this plane. Maybe we'll get some the next time a transport brings a load here."

One of the grease monkeys wears goggles over his eyes and carries a tool with flame at its end. He brings the edges of two pieces of metal together and heats them with the flame. The edges melt and make one piece where the two edges have been.

The men examine the plane all over. They are very careful, for they know that the lives of the pilot and crew depend upon them.

Jay and his helpers take the big engine apart. They use one tool after another as they put in new parts. When Jay needs new parts which he does not have, he cleans the bent or broken parts, straightens or mends them, and puts them back into the motor. Soon the men's faces and hands are covered with spots of grease. Another mechanic works on the machine gun. All of the men are busy on the plane.

The grease monkeys hear the noise of guns and bursting shells. Sometimes they must run for shelter when bombs begin to fall too near. But they work as steadily as they can so that the plane will soon be ready to fly.

"There," says Jay, turning to one of the busy mechanics, "my part is done. As soon as you fellows finish your work, Mark and the Dragon can take off."

In the meantime other transport planes land at the field. More mechanics and more supplies are brought in. The edges of the field are crowded with men unloading the supplies and working on planes.

But the grease monkeys are too busy to look up. They go over every part of Mark's plane to see if anything is wrong with it. They know that the pilots must have their planes put in good order.

Now the mechanics stand back from the plane. "O. K.?" asks Jay.

"O. K.," answer the others.

They watch while Mark takes off. When they see that the plane is running all right, they move on to begin work on a heavy bomber.

All day and well into the night they work on without stopping. As soon as planes land on the field, grease monkeys begin work on them. There are not enough mechanics to do all the work which is needed. They do not have all the airplane parts they need. Sometimes they take a wrecked plane apart to get the parts they need for another plane. Sometimes wrecked planes are put on a ship and sent back to our factories. The mechanics also need many more tools than they have, but they do as good work as they can without the tools.

This airfield which the paratroopers captured has already become an important air base of the Allies. United States planes can now land on its runways. Its hangars have been rebuilt. There are many cans of gasoline and other supplies for the planes. But the planes would not be ready for the pilots if it were not for the work of the mechanics. No one knows this better than the pilots. They are proud of the work the mechanics do. The success of the pilots and even their lives depend on the good work of the grease monkeys.

A Flying Transport

In another part of the world Frank Dixon and his crew take off in the afternoon sun. Frank has a load of airplane parts and big cans of gasoline to take across enemy country to one of our Allies. The trip ahead of the men is dangerous. They must travel over high mountains which are sometimes hidden by banks of clouds.

As the plane rises from the ground, it

Here is a fast transport which has four engines. Where are the engines? This plane can cross our country in less than nine hours without stopping. It is used to carry heavy loads swiftly. What can you tell about its landing gear?

creaks and seems as heavy as lead. Frank is carrying a big load because the supplies are badly needed. Our Ally cannot fight the enemy without them.

It is the first time that Tom Smith has ridden with Frank. Tom has business in the country of this Ally.

"This is always a hard trip," says Frank. "The weather is usually bad on this route. We may meet enemy planes along the way, and we've got only Tommy guns. They can't hit anything far away." Frank has such a heavy load of supplies that his plane cannot take bombs and machine guns to protect itself.

"I should think the clouds and bad weather would help you out," replies Tom.

"Yes, they do, but they make our flight dangerous, too. Enemy planes can come close without our knowing. We must have sharp eyes, but we'll need lots of luck, too."

Now the plane is high in the air. Just a little way below are mountaintops covered with snow. Big clouds are all around the plane.

Suddenly the radio man passes a message up to Frank.

" Enemy planes within forty miles," it says. Frank knows that the planes can reach him in only a few minutes.

Soon one of the crew calls out that he sees an enemy plane. Higher and higher Frank flies. But the plane has such a heavy load that it does not rise fast.

Now a swift enemy plane appears, and another, and another. They fly in formation and will soon overtake Frank's plane.

Frank ducks into the clouds. All around it looks like a white sea. The men see nothing. The windows look as if they were covered with white cotton. Still the heavy plane keeps climbing. Frank has got away from the enemy planes in the clouds.

In a few minutes Frank can go no higher. He has no oxygen masks for his men. You remember when a plane is flying high in the air, the men must breathe oxygen from a tank in the plane. In trying to get away from the enemy Frank has lost his way among the clouds. He hopes that he is flying so high that he will not run into one of the mountaintops.

As the co-pilot looks around, he sees a line of peaks, or sharp mountaintops. He studies his maps to find out where they are. But he cannot seem to tell, for the plane is not on its route.

The day gets darker, and Frank sees that the gasoline is low. The men in the plane begin to think about what may happen if they come down in enemy country. They feel their parachute straps to be sure they are fastened.

On and on the plane flies, but it seems to Frank that the clouds are everywhere. He cannot get away from them. Though he has flown this route many times, everything is strange to him. At last he-sees a sharp mountain peak which he knows. It looks like a finger pointing up into the sky.

"There's the field," shouts Frank, pointing down to a clear space between the mountains. "It is the place where we land.

"We won't have to land in enemy country this trip."

As the plane flies lower and lower, rain begins to fall. But there below, the men see an airfield in the midst of a thick forest. As Frank comes down to land on the wet runway, the wheels hit pools of water and send spray up into the air. The plane rolls up to the hangar and stops.

As the men tell their story to other transport crews on this same route, the supplies are unloaded.

Another load of air freight has been

The men are loading this transport with cargo. It can carry a big load. How is the cargo packed before it is put into the plane? Into what part of the plane do you think it is loaded?

brought safely to our Ally. Frank's plane has no fighter planes to protect it as some transports do. But he knows how much the supplies are needed. It is his job to bring them to this Ally, even though the route is dangerous.

When the plane returns to the American base, it will carry sick and wounded soldiers. Or it may carry a load of something which the Americans need.

Barrage Balloons Go Up

Don Eliot lives near an airfield just outside a big city on the east coast of the United States. He has a crew of eleven men who help him protect this airfield. They work with big balloons to keep enemy planes away.

Near by are many factories which make airplanes and jeeps. The enemy would like to bomb the factories. But Don and his men know how to work these big balloons to keep the enemy from attacking the city.

Over seventy balloons are kept on this field. They look like big flying fish. But Don and his crew call them "pigs."

The balloons are barrage balloons. No one rides in them. Part of the balloon is filled with gas. When the men send a balloon up, another part fills with air.

Acme Photo Service

These men are sending a barrage balloon up. The man inside the wire cage runs a machine which lets a wire rope underneath the balloon unwind like a kite string. It lets the balloon rise in the air. It does not take long for the balloon to go up. The people at one end of the field are watching to see the balloon rise. Why do you think the balloons are sent up from an open field?

The men must be able to send the barrage balloons up into the air. If enemy
planes are coming toward the city, Don
and his men must work quickly. They
might even have to work under fire.
They know how to get the balloons up
and how to bring them down again.

Today some new men are learning to
send the balloons up. Don and the rest
of the crew are working as carefully as if
they knew the enemy was coming. They
get into their places on the field. There
is a strong wire, or cable, fastened to each
balloon. The wire is wound on a big
spool, like a spool of thread. As the men
let the spool turn, the wire is unrolled,
and the balloon rises in the air.

As the balloon rises, Don and his men
are as careful of the cable as a fisherman
holding his line. They must not let the
balloon rise too fast because the wire

might break. They must not let the wind pull it away from them. If a big balloon got loose, its cable could damage electric wires and buildings near the field. The balloon might travel some distance before it came down.

Soon all the balloons are up in the air. Some of them are a mile above the field. Others are lower down.

Now if enemy planes try to dive down, they will run into the wires. The wires might cut off a wing or cut the plane in two, or wire might get tangled in the pro-peller blades of the plane.

A pilot diving down from above cannot see where the wires are. He is coming too fast. If he stays high up above the balloons, it will not be as easy to drop his bombs on the right targets.

But our planes must be careful, too, in places where there are barrage balloons.

The pilots must keep their planes away from the wires.

We use barrage balloons to protect important cities and ports from the enemy in time of war. These balloons protect factories where we are making things to use in war. We could keep airplanes flying about above our cities and factories and airports, but it would take many, many planes. It would cost too much to build enough airplanes to protect all the important places in our country.

Barrage balloons are sometimes fastened to trucks and moved about from place to place, where they are needed. They are sometimes fastened to ships at sea, too. One of our Allies sends barrage balloons up into the air above some of the ships in a convoy. Then it is hard for enemy planes to come near the ships to drop bombs.

Acme Photo Service

This balloon is being taken to the place where it is needed. What are the men traveling in? What keeps the balloon from getting loose?

197

The enemy would like to burn down our cities and to take pictures of them as they burn. But if enemy pilots come to these cities, men like Don and his crew will keep the barrage balloons in the air night and day. Enemy planes may get caught in the wires of the balloons. If they do not get caught, they will have to stay up so high that they will have little chance to hit important targets.

QUESTIONS TO TALK OVER

1. What kinds of places are planes sent to bomb as targets? Why?

2. How do paratroopers help us in a war?

3. What dangers do paratroopers meet?

4. What kind of work is done by a grease monkey with the Army Air Forces?

5. How important is a grease monkey's job? Give reasons for your answer.

6. Name ways in which we use our transport planes. See how many ways you can name.

7. How are barrage balloons used?

Things to Do

1. Make a drawing of an airport for army planes. In your picture show hangars, runways, and grease monkeys at work. Put all the drawings up where the class can see them. Then talk over which drawings best agree with the stories you have read.

2. Make a list of the ways in which paratroopers and smoke jumpers are alike and the ways in which they are different. Begin your list like this:

Alike	*Different*	
	Smoke jumpers:	Paratroopers:
a. jump from plane	a. fight fire	a. fight the enemy
b. take tools with them	b. are not fired at	b. may be fired at

3. Bring to school pictures which show airplanes at work. See how many of these pictures you can explain to your classmates. Collect the pictures showing one kind of work and put them up together. Place a title above these pictures.

Words to Explain

hangar	dropping zone	grease monkey
Allies	paratroopers	air base
Tommy gun	flares	barrage balloon

199

U. S. Coast Guard

This seaplane is guarding a convoy. Inside are observers watching for submarines. The pilot was told that the convoy was coming along the coast, and he went out to meet it. He will stay with the convoy as long as the ships are in the waters which this seaplane patrols. When the convoy leaves these waters, planes patrolling the next zone, or part of the sea, will watch over the convoy. In the picture you can see a big pontoon, or float, under the fuselage. There is a smaller pontoon under each wing. When the plane lands in water, the pontoon keeps it floating. Under each wing the plane carries bombs to drop on enemy submarines and blow them up.

CHAPTER VI

PLANES TODAY AND TOMORROW

What Planes Can Do

From the stories in this book you can see that traveling in a plane is different from traveling in an automobile or on a train. It is much easier to fly than to travel on the ground where there are many things which make it hard to move about. An airplane does not have to move along a road as an automobile does. A plane can travel above any kind of land, low or high, jungle or desert, dry or wet, slippery or rough. A plane can go almost anywhere in the air.

An automobile cannot go up a slope that is too steep for a road. An automobile cannot travel over land that is covered with trees and bushes. If the land is wet, the wheels of the car will sink down into it, and the driver cannot move his car. It is also hard for an automobile to travel over icy land. It cannot travel on water at all. A plane can travel above water, and a seaplane can land on water. Planes can also travel much faster than automobiles.

Today we are using planes in many ways. As you know, they transport passengers, mail, and express. They carry cargo which must go a long distance in a short time or which must go to places that are hard to reach by truck, railroad, or ship.

Planes help us to fight forest fires which would burn down many fine trees that we need for lumber. They carry food and supplies to men who patrol our forests in fire weather.

They carry food, medicines, doctors, and nurses to places which have been flooded or have met with other disasters. In time of floods pilots fly over the flooded land to see where people may be, on roof tops, in trees, or on bridges. The fliers plan ways of rescuing the people. They drop food and supplies to people who are safe on high ground with water all around them.

In a plane we can move an injured or sick person quickly to a hospital even though he is in a far-off place where there are no doctors and nurses.

Explorers can travel by plane to parts of the world where few people have ever been. They see what these places are like and come back to tell us. We use planes, too, when we want to make air photographs or quickly make a map of part of a country.

Perhaps you know that planes are used to bring flowers, fruits, and other foods to our big cities. If the flowers traveled by train, they would wither before they reached our flower shops. Many foods would have to be carried in refrigerator trains. But planes can bring food from different parts of our country in only a few hours.

Planes also help us to save our crops from insects which would eat the stems and leaves. The plane carries a hopper, or big box, full of a powder that poisons such insects. The hopper has openings in the bottom through which the pilot can drop the powder from the plane. Early in the morning when the plants are wet with dew, the pilot flies back and forth across the fields not far above the plants. As he flies, he moves a part of the hopper, and the powder drops down on the plants.

The powder sticks to the wet leaves and stems of the plants. When the insects eat the leaves, they are poisoned and die. The plane does this work quickly. If the farmer had to scatter the powder by hand, it would take him many days. If he scattered the powder only when the plants were wet with dew, he could cover only a small part of the field before the dew dried off. On mornings when there was no dew, he could not scatter the powder. The insects could do much harm to his fields.

In these stories you have read about the many ways planes help us during a war. Our pilots fly over the enemy's country to see what the enemy is doing. Our bombardiers and gunners destroy enemy troops, supplies, railroads, and aircraft. Big transport planes carry men and supplies to our battle fronts. Photographers fly over enemy country to take pictures of towns which have been bombed.

Before many years have passed, our engineers can spend their time learning how to build new kinds of planes. The new planes will help us in many ways which we do not know about today.

The Helicopter

Engineers are planning small planes which anyone will be able to fly. Before long we may ride around in the air in helicopters just as we ride along our highways in automobiles. Our factories may build helicopters to sell at a low price. Then many families will be able to buy them.

Though a helicopter is a heavier-than-air craft, it is not like other planes. A helicopter has no wings on its body. It has two propellers, a big one on top called

Consolidated Vultee Aircraft Corporation

Find the two rotors on this helicopter. What does the front of the helicopter look like? This helicopter has pontoons so that it can land on water or on the deck of a ship. It can land on the ground, too.

the rotor and a small one on the tail. The big propeller lifts the helicopter in the air and moves it through the air. The small propeller is used in steering, or guiding, the plane, so that it can go in any direction the pilot wishes.

Some helicopters have already been

built. In a two-place helicopter there is a seat in the cabin for the pilot and one other person. But later on helicopters may be built with enough seats for a big family.

When a helicopter takes off, it does not need a runway. Its big rotor revolves and lifts the machine straight up into the air. Then the pilot can fly forward or backward or sideways.

As you know, the planes which we use today travel very fast. They cannot move slowly in the air or stop in one place. But a helicopter can move very slowly. It can even stand in the air without moving. So if you are on a vacation trip in a helicopter, you can stop to look at a park or a beautiful mountain scene. You may want to watch a football game or a boat race.

When the pilot wishes to land, he does

not need a runway. His plane does not come down on a runway and taxi to its hangar. The helicopter comes straight down just as it goes straight up. It needs only enough space for its big rotor to turn without hitting anything.

The helicopter will be used in many ways. You and your family may go out riding in it on Sunday. People will ride to and from work in their helicopters. This means that they may live out in the country much farther from their work than they do today. When it is time for a man to go to work, he will fly from his home and land on the roof of the building where he works. In the evening he will take the elevator to the roof. He will climb into the pilot's seat, and start the rotors of the helicopter whirling. Then away he will fly to his home in the country.

The helicopter may be used as an air taxi. Then a man will call a helicopter when he wants to go to an airport. When he gets out, he will pay the pilot for the ride. When a passenger comes into an airport on a big air liner, he will call a helicopter taxi to take him to a hotel. The pilot of the taxi will put the man's suitcase in, and off they will fly. On the roof of the hotel where the helicopter lands, the man will pay for his ride. A porter will take his suitcase, and they will take an elevator down to the office. Then the man can ask for a room.

If helicopters are built large enough for many people to ride in them, they may be used as air buses.

Helicopters are being used today in our Army Air Forces. These helicopters carry messages from near the battle front back to headquarters. If the pilot drops a telephone line down to the ground, he does not have to land to give his message.

Because the helicopter does not need running space, it is a good plane to use at sea. It can land on a ship which does not have a flight deck, if the deck is large enough to allow for the big rotor.

In a helicopter injured persons may be rescued from places which are hard to reach. If a plane crashes into a thick jungle, it might take many days to reach the crew by traveling on the ground. A plane could not land in such a place unless there were a landing field near by. But a helicopter could come straight down in a small clearing in the jungle. The crew would place the injured person in the helicopter, which could then fly to a hospital. All of this would take but a short time.

A family owning a helicopter will want

U. S. Army Air Corps

This helicopter stands still above the ground while a girl hands a bundle up to a man who is riding with the pilot. The man opens the door to take the bundle. This plane has wheels instead of pontoons. It is made to land on the ground.

to keep the machine near the place where they live. Then they can get into it quickly when they want to go riding, and they can land at home after their ride. A helicopter might be kept in a big back yard, or a small hangar could be built for it there. People could whir up into the air from their back yards.

Perhaps people who live in big apartment houses will keep their helicopters on the roof. Or an upper story of the building might be used as a hangar for many helicopters. Elevators could lift the helicopters from the upper story to the roof.

But when many, many people pilot planes, we shall need to follow safety rules. Before a person takes a helicopter up, he must know that it is in good working order. He must know how to run his machine. He must see that it does not get in the way of other planes. We should not like to have traffic jams in the air as we often have on the ground. The pilot must land and take off in the right places. Maybe we shall have air policemen to see that everyone who flies a plane follows the rules of the air.

Today many people who would like to

213

own planes do not have them because of the high cost. Even a small plane costs much more than an ordinary automobile. It is also expensive to have mechanics care for a plane, and new parts cost a good deal. But if thousands and thousands of simple planes such as the helicopter should be made in our factories, the machines would cost much less. Then many families might own planes. We would see small planes as often as we see automobiles. The more planes were built, the cheaper they would become. Soon they might not cost any more than an automobile.

The Flying Automobile

Of course the helicopter is not the only plane which may be built for people who wish to fly a small plane. Already engineers are at work planning different kinds of flying automobiles. Pilots are trying out these cars to see if anything is wrong with them and how they may be made better.

Sometimes several engineers work together in designing a new plane. The men try to plan the new planes so that they will not be expensive to make. They try out new materials to see whether planes made of those materials are strong enough to carry passengers and cargo. Engineers try to plan new planes so that they will not need a great deal of gasoline to make the motors run. Every time a new plane is made, pilots test it to see how good it is. After they have flown the new plane for a while, they take it to pieces to test each part. It takes many men to design and build a new plane and then to test the plane in the air.

Consolidated Vultee Aircraft Corporation

This drawing shows how a man could let down the flying parts onto an air car. The wings and tail will be fastened to the car. Then after the man has left the hangar, he will be able to fly up into the sky.

Some men who have built airplanes for many years are working on a flying car in which people can take short pleasure trips. This car is only about half as heavy as a small coupe. It can travel sixty to seventy miles an hour on the road and uses about as much gasoline as an ordinary automobile.

Our engineers are trying to make flying cars so safe that anyone can pilot them. A man will not have to be a trained pilot to fly safely in these small planes.

For a flying trip, the pilot drives the car to the airport. Here he lets down from the hangar roof the wings and tail of his car. They are hooked on, and a propeller is fastened to the rear of the body. After the driver takes off, he can travel in the air about a hundred miles an hour. And he can carry enough gasoline to go as far as from Chicago to Detroit.

People who live on the plains where big towns are far apart will perhaps want a plane which can travel farther than these flying autos. They will need a plane which can carry enough gasoline for a long trip. For these people a machine is being built and tried out. It is really a plane, but it can also travel on a road. It is called a " roadable " airplane.

The roadable plane does not weigh as much as the flying auto. This means it can travel faster in the air. When it travels on the ground, its wings are folded back. On the ground it goes about thirty-five miles an hour.

If the weather gets stormy when a pilot is traveling in his roadable plane, he can land. Then he can fold his wings and travel on the ground.

Consolidated Vultee Aircraft Corporation

This drawing shows how we may be able to travel someday. The helicab will be able to move in any direction or to stand still in the air. The pilot and passengers will be able to see out on all sides. This helicab will be able to land on a rooftop. The big rotor on top of the helicab is turning around and around. You can see another helicab on the other side of the yard. Its rotor is not moving. Some helicabs will have pontoons instead of wheels. Where would a helicab with pontoons be used?

In this new kind of car, the passengers see everything around them. The car is built with a rounded front where the driver and passengers sit. The front is made of a material which you can see through as you see through glass.

219

Within a few years we shall have cheap sky machines which do not weigh much and are easy to fly. Men want to make it possible for people to talk from one plane to another, and from a plane to someone on the ground. When many people are flying, they must be careful not to run into other planes.

The Stratosphere Plane

For a long time our big airlines have been making plans to improve passenger planes. They want new kinds of planes which can travel very fast and carry many more passengers than our planes of today can.

Today our passenger planes are sometimes delayed by fog and storms. At times the weather is so stormy that it is not safe for the planes to take off. Sometimes they must come down before they reach the end of their journey. Then the passengers wait in the airport for the weather to get clear, or they take a train to the place where they are going.

There is a part of the sky six or seven miles up where the weather is never stormy or cloudy, but where the winds blow steadily and at great speed. We call this part of the sky the stratosphere. Planes can travel very fast in the strato-sphere, where they are blown along by the swift winds.

As you know, the air gets thin farther and farther away from the earth. The stratosphere has such thin air that it does not contain enough oxygen for us to breathe. If anyone goes into the strato-sphere, he must wear an oxygen mask or have more oxygen to breathe.

Our airlines are designing special kinds of planes for stratosphere flying.

This drawing shows a kind of passenger plane we may sometime have. How do the passengers enter this plane? How is it different from our passenger planes of today?

These planes will travel much faster than any planes we have today. They will travel on non-stop flights across our country and to distant countries.

Stratosphere planes will carry fifty passengers or even more. They will need a larger crew to run the plane than our passenger planes have today.

After passengers get on a stratosphere plane, the doors will be sealed. The plane will be built in such a way as to be airtight. The windows will perhaps be of double glass. The air between the panes will help to keep the cold from getting into the plane.

Even though the weather outside is far below zero, it will be warm and comfortable in the plane. Oxygen will be added to the air so that the crew and passengers will not have to breathe through masks. The air will be heated so that passengers can breathe as easily as when they are on the ground.

The stratosphere plane will have more than one deck. There will be dining rooms in which meals will be served to the passengers. There will be pleasant sitting

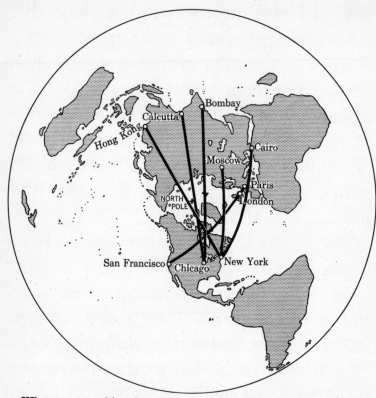

When we travel by plane, we can reach other places in the world much more quickly than ever before. Of course, planes move faster than ships, automobiles, or trains. But planes also can travel by the shortest routes. See the short routes to distant places which are shown on this map.

224

rooms in which passengers may work and play during the day. There will be many separate cabins, or bedrooms, for the passengers.

In the nose and sides of the stratosphere plane there will be windows for the passengers to look through. In the daytime they may see mountains and lakes far below. On a clear night they will see the stars and perhaps the beam of a beacon light moving over the sky.

Since there are no storms in the stratosphere, the plane will ride smoothly. Riding in a stratosphere plane will be the fastest way that anyone can travel. By traveling with helping winds, far above stormy weather, the plane will go faster than our passenger planes of today.

Of course, a stratosphere plane will be able to travel all around the world. But every country in the world owns the air above its land. It has the right to say whether planes can fly over its land. So we cannot send our planes over other countries and cannot land in those countries until our government has asked the other governments if we may. Our government and the governments of other countries will perhaps make laws that will allow passenger planes to travel around the world and make stops at certain places.

Men are making plans for our stratosphere planes to fly across the North Pole. This is a much shorter way to go to some lands than to fly across the ocean. The stratosphere plane will fly so fast that people may visit distant places even on short vacations.

The Flying Wing

Engineers are talking about planes which will look very different from those we see today in the sky. Some of the designs for these planes show a very big wing. Our planes of today have a body with wings fastened to it.

The flying wing looks from the front like a wide V. The point of the V is the nose of the plane. At the back of the plane are the propellers. There are no propellers at the front. This wing is so large that it must be run by much more powerful engines than most of our planes need today. These engines are built inside the wing. The three wheels on which this new plane lands are drawn up into the wing when the plane is flying.

The flying wing will carry hundreds of passengers. It will be a comfortable plane to travel on, too. There will be dining rooms, cabins, a dance floor, card rooms, a deck for passengers to walk on, and other comforts. Light and sunshine will come in through curved windows in the upper surface of the wing and along the edges.

The flying wing will travel very fast, either in the stratosphere or just below it. Maybe it will take only about half as long to cross our country as our present planes do.

As our engineers learn more and more about how to build aircraft, they change their plans and make better planes. So we can expect to have better and better planes in the years to come.

Sky Freighters

Today our factories are building huge transport planes to rush cargo to distant places in the world. Transport planes are being built larger and larger. Soon they may be built as high as a two-story house, and with much longer bodies and wings than any planes that we have seen.

Engineers are designing these planes with wide doors to shove freight through. A gasoline tank truck will not go through the doors of ordinary planes. It can be carried in them only if it is taken apart. Then when it reaches the end of its journey, the parts have to be put together again. Men must work a long time before the truck is ready to use.

But if the truck were carried on a plane built to transport trucks, it could be loaded in a few minutes. A wide platform would be rolled near the plane. Men would lay it firmly from the ground to the door of the plane. Then a driver would get into the truck and guide it right up this platform into the plane.

More and more, our engineers are designing special planes for different kinds of cargo.

This drawing shows the kind of transport plane we may have someday. Cargo will be rolled into the plane from a platform. The small drawing shows how the plane looks up in the sky. What differences do you see between this plane and the transports which are shown in other pictures in this book?

Men are also beginning to study how to load planes. Our boxcars, as you know, are loaded by men who know how. Some have learned how to pack furniture for railroad transportation and how to load it into box cars so that it will not be broken. Others know just how to pack

230

boxes of fruits and vegetables so that they will travel in good condition.

If the cargo of a plane is not packed just right, it may be damaged on the trip.

Also, when the cargo is poorly packed, space will be left inside the plane. Then the plane will not be able to carry as heavy a load as it should. Part of the cargo will have to be left behind.

Today men from airplane factories and others who know how to load and ship cargo are working together to find out the best ways to load planes. They are studying how to box or wrap up things which are to be carried. Many things which are carried on the ground in box cars are placed in a wooden frame, or crate. But the crates take up space that might be used for other cargo. Lumber is heavy, too. So the men are trying to find ways of wrapping up much of the cargo in packages and fastening the packages inside the plane.

People are also trying to work out easy ways of lifting heavy cargo into a plane and of packing it inside the plane. They try to see that all the space is used up, and that there are no empty spaces. The cargo should be packed so that it will be easy to unload, too.

It is also important to get the freight to the airport the quickest and easiest way possible. In the past it has sometimes taken a long time to transport freight to a near-by airport. The freight was put on a truck at the factory where it was made. Then it was carried to the railroad yards, packed in a box car, moved closer to the airport, taken off, packed in another truck, and then carried to the airport. Today men are working out ways of moving freight from the factory right to the airport.

Press Association, Inc

See this glider being loaded for a trip across the ocean. It will carry boxes of radio and airplane parts. What part of the glider have the men opened up to put the load in? A transport plane will tow this glider through the air.

Maybe our transport planes will soon pull several gliders which also carry cargo. A glider has a pilot and is heavier than air like an airplane. But it does not have a motor. It is pulled, or towed,

233

behind the plane like the trailer of an automobile. It is not so heavy as a plane and has more space for carrying freight. It does not cost as much to build as a plane. Of course, we want to move air freight as cheaply as possible.

A plane speeding by an airport can pick up a glider without stopping. The glider is fastened to the plane with a tow line. A plane can also let a glider land at an airport while the plane keeps going. The plane lets go of the glider, and then the pilot of the glider guides it to the landing field.

So you see gliders save much time. The plane does not have to land to deliver the glider's load.

Our transport planes are carrying heavier and heavier loads and traveling the shortest and quickest routes through the sky.

Airports and Flight Strips

As time goes on, there will be more air traffic between our cities than we have ever seen. The many planes which American families will own will be taking off and landing. There will be air taxis, buses, and big passenger planes. Giant transport planes will be carrying goods back and forth. Some planes will travel short distances to bring cargo to a main airline and to take cargo back to small towns. There will also be planes which large companies will use in their business. All these planes will need airports from which to take off and on which to land.

There will probably be different kinds of airports for the different planes. The very large planes which carry freight and supplies will need airports with long runways. Engineers are trying to work out ways for a big plane to make a shorter run before rising into the air. Maybe men will find some safe way of shooting it into the air. The airport will need to be built so that planes can land and take off very quickly. Then many planes can use the same runways. Many men will be needed at the airport to handle the large cargoes which come in and out, just as many men are needed at railroad freight stations today.

Airports for passenger planes will also have many runways so that planes can arrive and leave quickly. Perhaps some of the larger planes which men and women own will also land at these airports. Around the landing field will be hotels, restaurants, and gas stations. Then people who fly their own planes can stop off easily for a meal or overnight.

Flight strips will also be built. They

are landing places with only one runway. They will be used mostly by people who live near by. Some of these strips have already been built along main roads. The road is widened, or another strip of road is built beside it. There will be thousands of these strips, and they will be built in places where many people want to land.

New Ways of Traveling

Today many people who live in our cities drive a long way every morning to reach the places where they work. In the evening they drive home again. They like to live far away from the busy part of the town and are willing to spend much time driving back and forth.

Before long, people can live much farther away from their work than they do now. They will have small planes of their own and will fly to work. Many people may live in the country, away from the city where they work.

On week ends people can go on trips to distant places. They can cross our country from the Atlantic to the Pacific Ocean or from the Great Lakes to the Gulf of Mexico.

On a two-week vacation we can travel to any place in the world. We will come to know other peoples and the ways they live. We will learn to eat their foods and to play their games. We will see the kinds of work they do. Maybe they will come to our country to see how we live. Then the people of different countries will not seem like strangers to each other. It will be easy for different peoples to learn to know each other when they can travel quickly by air. There is no place where airplanes will not fly.

Questions to Talk Over

1. Why has it been said that we live in the flying forties?

2. How does an airplane differ from an automobile?

3. Which would you rather own, a helicopter or a flying automobile? Why?

4. How does a helicopter differ from other planes?

5. Why are some airlines planning to build and use stratosphere planes?

6. How do airplane builders work to make their planes better?

7. What differences in our lives will come from new ways of traveling by air?

Things to Do

1. Make a list of all the ways in which we will use new kinds of planes. Begin your list like this:

Uses

a. Carrying cargo.

b. Going on vacation trips.

2. Make a picture of one of these planes:

A helicopter

A roadable plane

A stratosphere plane

A big transport plane with a train of gliders

The class may examine each picture to see which one agrees best with the stories you have read.

3. Make a list of all the ways that people may travel in the next ten years. Begin your list like this:

Ways to Travel

a. In an automobile

b. In a helicopter

Then talk over in class which ways of travel are fast and which are slow. Are there times when traveling slowly is better than traveling fast? Why?

4. Bring to school as many pictures of airports as you can find. Study the pictures to see whether or not these will be good airports for the new kinds of planes. Write a paragraph explaining what changes you think will be needed in these airports.

WORDS TO EXPLAIN

helicopter	stratosphere	stratosphere plane
rotor	glider	tow line
flying automobile	flying wing	flight strip
roadable plane	sky freighter	design (for a plane)

engineer, man who plans and builds engines; an inventor.

explode, burst with a loud noise.

explorer, a traveler who goes into new or unknown places to see what he can find there.

express, packages carried by a company which transports such goods.

expressman, man who works in the express business.

F

flash, appear suddenly.

flood, overflow of water on the land. When water rises high in a river, it may flow over the land and cause a flood.

fog, thick mist. In a heavy fog one can see only a little way even though it is daytime.

formation, arrangement; pattern. When planes fly in a group, each plane in its place, we say the planes fly in formation. They make a pattern in the sky.

fuselage, body of a plane. The wings and the tail are fastened to the fuselage.

G

galley, place where the cooking is done on a plane or ship or where the food is served. A galley is like a small kitchen.

glide, move smoothly and without noise. When a plane glides, its engine is not running.

glider, heavier-than-air flying machine without an engine.

glisten, sparkle; shine.

grove, a small wood. A grove does not have as many trees as a forest.

gunner, one who has charge of a gun.

H

hangar, shed for aircraft.

harness, cords, straps, or other trappings worn by a man for his protection or by an animal that is to be driven. An aviator's harness holds his parachute in place.

hatchet, small axe with a short handle. A hatchet is used with one hand.

helicopter, airplane which can go straight up and come down without using a runway. The propeller is on top instead of in front.

helium, a light gas which will not burn. Helium is used to fill balloons.

helmet, a covering to protect a person's head. Some helmets also protect the face and neck.

I

inspect, look over; examine.

island, a piece of land having water all around it.

J

jungle, place covered thickly with grass, bushes, and trees

L

launch, 1. set going. 2. set out.

level, in a straight line.

lookout, 1. person who keeps watch. 2. place from which the watch is kept.

lumber, wood sawed into boards; timber ready for use.

M

manager, one who directs or guides a business.

mask, a covering to protect or to hide the face. Children wear masks on Hallowe'en. A ball player wears a mask to protect his face.

mechanic, man who takes care of machines. A mechanic may work on the engine of an automobile or a plane.

microphone, an instrument into which a radio operator speaks.

midnight, twelve o'clock at night.

movable, able to be moved.

mule, an animal that looks like a horse but has longer ears. A mule can carry a heavy load and will not slip on a steep path.

N

napkin, small cloth which a person uses at the table to wipe his hands and lips and to keep from soiling his clothes.

O

observer, one whose work it is to watch.

officer, person who holds a position of command in an army or navy. He has men under him.

overlap, spread over; partly cover.

overnight, during the night.

overtake, catch up with.

oxygen, a gas which is in the air we breathe and without which we cannot live. Oxygen has no color or smell.

P

pajamas, a sleeping suit having loose trousers and a jacket.

parachute, a pack worn by an aviator to help him jump with safety from a plane. When a parachute is opened up, it looks like a huge umbrella. It slows down one's fall from a plane. Parachutes are also fastened to bundles which are dropped from planes.

paratrooper, soldier who is trained to jump safely from a plane by using a parachute.

244

passenger, person traveling in a plane, train, ship, or the like.

patrol, travel over a place for guarding or protecting it; as, the policeman patrolled the street in an automobile.

periscope, instrument used in submarines through which things above the surface of the water can be seen when the submarine is below the water.

photographer, one who takes photographs. A photographer makes his living by taking pictures.

pilot, person who flies an aircraft.

port, harbor for ships; sheltered place or waterway near a coast. Boats come into port when they are to be loaded or unloaded.

propeller, part of an airplane that turns fast and drives the plane forward.

R

raft, float formed of logs fastened together. When men are shipwrecked at sea, they often float on a raft. Sometimes rafts are made of rubber so that they may be filled with air.

ranger, man who cares for a forest.

refrigerator, a cooler for food. Refrigerator cars are used to transport fresh meats, fruits, and vegetables.

regular, usual.

remaining, left; the rest.

report, tell about.

rescue, save from danger.

restaurant, place to buy and eat meals.

revolve, turn round and round

rip-cord, a strong string which, when pulled, jerks a parachute out of its pack. A person jerks the rip-cord when he wishes to open his parachute.

roadable, able to travel on a road.

roll, in an airplane, tilt from one side to the other, putting one wing higher than the other. A pilot rolls his plane to put it into a bank.

rotor, propeller; revolving part on a helicopter.

route, way.

runway, ground which a plane travels over in taking off or in landing.

rustle, make soft sounds, as of the moving of dry leaves.

S

scene, view. A picture of life in the country shows a country scene.

seaplane, airplane which can rise from water and come down upon water.

slope, hillside; land slanting downward.

245

smolder, burn without flame.

speed, go fast; hurry.

squadron, group, usually made up of nine planes.

stewardess, young woman who looks after the passengers on a plane. She is sometimes called the hostess.

stratosphere, upper part of the atmosphere, six or seven miles up, where there is little water, swift winds, and weather which is always the same.

streamer, narrow piece of ribbon fastened to one end of a kite, parachute, or the like; the other end of the ribbon is free.

submarine, a ship which can travel under the water as well as on top of the water.

suitcase, traveling bag. A man can carry a suit of clothes in his suitcase.

supplies, provisions. School supplies are those things which pupils and teachers need in their school work. Army supplies are those things which an army needs such as food, guns, and bullets.

surface, top; outside.

sway, swing; move back and forth.

T

target, mark to shoot at.

taxi, 1. a taxicab, or automobile that can be hired. 2. move over the ground or water. A plane taxis to get into the right position for rising.

terminal, end. The end of a railroad line with its stations and sheds is a terminal.

torpedo, a weapon dropped from an airplane or fired from a submarine to blow up ships.

trail, 1. path through a place where bushes or trees grow wild; as, a trail through a forest. 2. that which trails; as, a line of smoke. As a burning plane falls, it may leave a trail of smoke in the air.

transport, carry. A transport plane is one used to carry cargo.

troops, soldiers.

tube, hollow instrument for carrying a gas or a liquid. The straw through which one drinks soda is a tube.

U

underbrush, bushes, small trees, and other plants which grow under large trees in a forest· brush.

V

vapor, mist; anything which floats in the air and makes it less clear; as, smoke, fog, or steam.

W

weary, tired; worn out.

246

INDEX

247